MW01196248

SCRAMBLED

*The secrets of leadership under extreme pressure
that I used on September 11, 2001
and how you can use them in business, life and combat*

by
Martin Richard

*To Skip!
CHECK 6.
opus*

CONTENTS

PREFACE

I was SCRAMBLED on September 11, 2001. I was SCRAMBLED in my F-15 Eagle, SCRAMBLED in the seemingly uncontrollable cascade of thoughts flying through my mind, and SCRAMBLED in the emotional morass conjured by the worst terrorist attacks perpetrated on American soil and my proximity to them. The United States Air Force had spent well over $25 million dollars training me to make the right decision under the most stressful conditions imaginable, but I had never felt so ill prepared and apprehensive about a mission as I did that perilous day. On the night of September 11th, I sat in silent, lonely darkness reflecting on the day. What I realized was that the secret to performing a highly stressful mission, and being an effective leader under pressure was something found deep inside of me already. It was a simple foundational tenet of the high performance culture I grew up and matured in, but it was twisted, convoluted, and hidden by the stress of the situation. How does stress and uncertainty in your life affect your ability to perform on the job? How does it reach into and interact in your personal relationships. Is there a way to use existing techniques and methodologies to thrive in stressful situations?

Remember back to the beginning of Operation Iraqi Freedom? While our Air Force flew combat missions over Iraq, the Iraqi Air Force didn't even try to get off of the ground. The reason they remained on the ground was simple: they couldn't compete, and they knew it. Wouldn't it be nice if your competition perceived your company as performing so well that they quaked in their boots every time they thought about going head-to-head with you? Let me show you how to create this environment. One key to evoking this "non-response" is to develop the skills to get the job done under stress. This book takes the millions of dollars the USAF has invested in me and puts it to work for you. Welcome to your stimulus package!

Have you started feeling the stress of a high-pressure situation, given this country's current economic, social, and political crises? How about on the job? Has the current environment reached your desktop, changing the way you approach day-to-day operations? Are you like me, and feeling the pressure affect the quality of life at home? Well, if you answered yes to any of these questions you are in good company!

It never ceases to amaze me that people think the resolution of a high-stress; high-pressure situation is in some degree left to chance. WRONG! The reason people are convinced that some or all of the components of a high-pressure situation are out of their control is because they don't have a method for dealing with them. All day long they deal with business challenges in a clear, methodical way, but when the pressure is on, people change their approach and lose their place. In my experience in combat and in business, this is a response to the stress created by the uncertainty of the situation. The result is that people jump into the execution stage of the business process to just "get it done," without any regard for a plan to produce the desired result. A perfect antidote to this response is a methodology I created that melds together my experiences in preparing for the most stressful combat missions, yet has a keen eye to the needs created by relentless business cycles.

Just as I was compelled to reflect on September 11th and the life changing events of that day, I hope this book will inspire you to think about how pressure and stress affect your life and how you can rise above them to make the best decision for you, your company, and your team. I challenge you to add to my ideas, use my techniques, and mold them to fit your situation. Share and ask questions. Try new approaches and in the process, humor me a bit; take on every high-pressure situation with a bit of attitude. By the end of our next few pages together, you'll see why anyone can be an effective leader in any high-pressure situation. Anyone.

ACKNOWLEDGEMENTS

This book is dedicated to my family: Kimberly, Rylan, and Christian for their relentless support, encouragement and love throughout this process! You Rock!

In the wings: Rita Richard, Leo and Elizabeth Richard, Brad, Patti and Ian Martin, James and Thomas Ginnetti, Ram Fullen and my mentor Sam Samsel.

To Duff: colleague, brother in arms, and friend. We built Fighter Associates from the ground up. It wouldn't have been as rich an experience without your knowledge.

I would like to acknowledge all of the people who helped me complete this book: To Abner, Kingpin, Heater, Rudy, LJ & Jill, Shaz and Nemo.

All the bro's in the 428th, 524th, 53rd Fighter Squadrons and the 102d Fighter Wing. To Norma! Thank you to the parents and staff of Pope John Paul II High School in Hyannis, Massachusetts and St Pius X School in South Yarmouth, Massachusetts.

Without ALL of you this would have just been another idea.

Disclaimer: The views in this book are those of the author and do not represent the views of the DoD, The Department of the Air Force or the Air National Guard.

Front cover photo of the World Trade Centers is from the National Oceanic and Atmospheric Administration/Department of Commerce collection and the National Parks Service.

Top back cover photo courtesy of Matthew Jackson. Cover photos of the mighty F15 is courtesy of Ken Middleton: http://www.102ndfighterwing.com

Bio Photo by Sandra Leigh: http://www.sandraleighphotos.com

Scrambled, copyright 2010, Martin Richard and Check 6 Racing, LLC

1

The Challenge:
Leadership under Extreme Pressure

"Standards set by precedent rarely suffice; I prefer to set my own."

—Anon

I. The Challenge: Leadership under Extreme Pressure

You don't always get to choose the conditions in which you will be called to be a leader—something I found out amid the smoke, twisted burning metal, and tears of September 11, 2001. That terrible day I was SCRAMBLED to intercept United Airlines Flight 93 and any other hijacked aircraft to prevent them from reaching their intended targets. My orders were simple and eerily straightforward: intercept, identify, divert, and if no response was received, then be prepared to shoot it down. And even though in the past I had been in the most dire and complex combat situations, these were absolutely the most ominous orders I had ever received.

I flew F-15 Eagles from Otis Air National Guard Base on Cape Cod, Massachusetts, the home of the 102nd Fighter Wing. For 35 years, the 102nd sat waiting anonymously to spring into action at a moment's notice on "alert." Organizationally, the Fighter Wing fell under Air Combat Command and worked closely with NORAD and the Northeast Air Defense Sector (NEADS), now the Eastern Air Defense Sector, to guard the skies of the northeast. Every day, 365 days a year, 24 hours a day, at least two fighter pilots and four maintenance personnel ate, slept, and lived nestled adjacent to three fully loaded F15 jets: their objective, to be airborne in 10 minutes or less if the "horn" went off. Sitting alert was akin to being a fireman. When the horn went off, no matter where I was or what I was doing, I had to swiftly don my anti-g suit, parachute harness, and helmet, run to the jet where my maintenance crew was waiting, fire up the powerful jet engines, and check all of the systems while simultaneously talking with the Otis Command Post who had a direct feed from NEADS. When the horn blew, a frantic, harrowing race into a high pressure situation ensued. The Command Post fed me pertinent information about the target, such as its altitude, heading, speed, and location. With that, I anxiously strapped in and taxied out of the hangar to take off. It was all I could do to control the rush of adrenaline coursing through my shaking body. The American public was largely oblivious to the alert mission. Historically, the role received notoriety during the peak of the Cold War, when Eagles from Otis were regularly sent skyward to intercept and escort Soviet bombers drifting up and down the east coast of the United States. This dangerous game of cat and mouse was practiced regularly on both sides of the globe. It was an unwelcome calling card, yet for the most part a benign action. When the Berlin Wall fell, the flights trickled off and eventually all but ceased, so the requirement to be on alert evolved into more of a focus on the transport of contraband.

Typically, drug interdiction missions occurred under cover of night over the dark, lonesome, churning Atlantic. We used night vision goggles to help us spot drug-running aircraft and covertly identify their route of flight. Being close to the ground at night and having to intercept slow-moving airplanes made these missions particularly complicated in the grand scheme of things. In the late 1990s and on through 2000, the alert mission languished. In fact, the last three times I pulled alert duty, I had been SCRAMBLED on a Coast Guard jet, which was based at Otis incidentally, a fish spotting airplane and believe it or not, a U.S. Navy Destroyer. My last three SCRAMBLES did not bode well for the ferocity of the mission's future or the stability of the command-and-control structure of the northeast. Budget cuts and unfashionable assignments threatened the alert mission at Otis up to September 10th. That was about to change with a vengeance.

September 11, 2001 was ordained by the United Nations as its "International Day of Peace." The fall morning's deep azure blue sky gave no indication of how the day would end. I was scheduled to complete a normal training mission in the F-15 Eagle, as I had done hundreds of times before. The dynamic environment of flying high-performance aircraft was my baseline—it was to some extent routine. My focus was on completing the training mission in the most effective and efficient manner. That day I was scheduled to participate in a Defensive Counter Air (DCA) mission. It featured four of our F-15s flying as "blue air," or the good guys, versus 4 on the "red air," or as adversaries. For blue air, this was a chance to hone their tactical training in a multi-bogey environment. In DCA, the goal is protect a point on the ground. Our training objective focused on ensuring flawless radar operations to be able to build an accurate picture of the threat's formation, target the threat in the most effective manner, and ensure, through mutual support, that all blue air forces returned unscathed. We also used the training to hone both our offensive employment and defensive maneuvering to stay alive. Tens of miles in front of the point we were protecting, the four-ship of F-15s maneuvered, targeted, and engaged the red air F-15s in this mock war scenario. It was an exciting sortie to do as a practice mission and it took a great deal of organization to make happen.

After the coordination briefing, I went to the Life Support shop to throw on all of my flying gear. The seven other pilots and I then gathered at the Operations Desk, where the Supervisor of Flying (SOF) for the day briefed us on current weather and airfield updates. He also gave us the status of the KC-135 air-to-air refueling jet, since getting fuel mid-flight was another part of the day's mission. Air-to-air refueling extended the time we could stay in the air to fight and afforded us the opportunity for more comprehensive training.

I arrived at the jet and completed the walk-around inspection, checked the jet's inspection forms, and spoke to the crew chief. Everything was good to go. As my jet rumbled to life and the enormous Pratt-Whitney PW-100 engines awoke, I noticed a commotion on one side of the flight line ramp. The broken, disjointed communication over the ultrahigh frequency (UHF) radio indicated confusion. Members of the 102nd Security Forces Squadron, the cops, marshaled into protective positions. Two vehicles appeared with their blue emergency lights flashing. We all knew what was going on: the alert aircraft were being

SCRAMBLED. I held my formation in the chocks to give way to the two jets that NORAD had summoned. I did not know that inside the squadron, there was absolute chaos.

Moments earlier, a phone call came to the Operations Desk. Master Sergeant Mark "G" Rose answered. He held the phone up to the senior alert pilot, Tim "Duff" Duffy and said, "Duff, it's for you. It's Otis tower—something about a hijacking."

In an Air Defense Unit, the term "hijacking" is not used glibly. Duff instructed Rose to transfer the call to the Command Post, where the call should have gone in the first place. Normally, the call would have gone from the FAA, via the military liaison, to NORAD and the chain of command would proceed, but this was no normal day.

Duff pulled the portable radio from his flight suit and said, "Alpha Kilo 1 and 2 suit up." He was leaning on his experience to be proactive and got the process of getting airborne going on his own. His intuition said something wasn't right. In fighter aviation, *Speed is Life.* He met Dan "Nasty" Nash in Life Support and they quickly dressed. Before leaving the squadron to go the alert facility where the jets sat waiting, Duff poked his cranium into the Command Post. Squadron Commander Jon "Tracer" Tracy was on two phones. He had one phone in each ear, speaking with NEADS on one phone and the FAA on the other simultaneously. This crude form of a communication bridge represented the technological link that initiated the war on terrorism. In a menacing tone, Tracer lifted his head and said, "Looks like it's real."

Like a flash, Duff and Nasty ran out of the squadron to the alert vehicle, jumped in, and sped to the "barns." As they drove to the alert facility about a half-mile away, the radio announced, "BATTLESTATIONS!" This command indicated two important things. First, it was the command to strap into the jet and prepare for further orders, but not to start engines. "Battlestations" served as a delicate balance between a high state of readiness and the need to conserve precious resources—fuel and oxygen. Second, it indicated that NORAD was in the loop since they were the command authority who would have to issue such an order.

Duff and Nasty hastily readied for their flight while they listened to the radios for information about their upcoming unplanned mission. The Command Post ordered, "RUNWAY ALERT," which meant the two F-15 pilots were to start their engines, check all of their systems, and taxi to the end of the runway, but to hold position there without launching. Runway Alert ratcheted up the readiness to an even higher state.

I watched from my jet as the clamshell doors on the alert hangars opened, heard the alert jets engines whine to life, and saw them aggressively emerge from the facility like an eager predator in search of its prey. Suddenly, the Command Post announced, "SCRAMBLE!" They blasted off, shattering the previously still, calm, peaceful morning.

Back on the flight line, I arranged my formation for takeoff and followed the standard procedures en route to our training area southwest of Martha's Vineyard. Everything was exceedingly normal until we heard some unfamiliar radio communication between Boston Center and some civilian airliners. It got my attention, but more because it was out of the norm, not because it was especially noteworthy. I commanded my formation to complete its pre-mission safety checks and readied them for the simulated war we had planned hours before. We entered our practice airspace, W-105, and commenced our tactical systems checks. I directed a g-force warm-up maneuver to prepare our bodies for the vigorous mission we had constructed. The g-force warm-up is analogous to the athlete's stretching before his game. We align our formation directly across from each other with about one mile spacing in-between jets. Then we accelerate in full afterburner and roll into approximately 80-85 degrees of bank. We aggressively pull on the stick and increase the g-force on the jet and our bodies. There is a physiological response in the body that actually helps us prepare for the high-g environment. After completing two of these practice turns, our minds and bodies were ready to fight. In preparation for the mission, I split the four jets simulating the red air to the west side of the airspace, while we took up position on the east side. About 80 miles separated us at the start of the fight. Just then, a controller from Boston Center called, "Slam 1, Boston Center."

"Go ahead," I responded curiously because for a controller to interrupt our training mission was out of the norm.

"Slam 1, an aircraft just crashed into the World Trade Center and I think you should return to base immediately," he said.

"Copy," meaning I understood; still, I was a bit confused. I didn't know the extent of the pandemonium residing just outside of our sterile training airspace. The Boston Center controller already knew what I would find out in a few moments. He was being proactive. Something told him this action was intentional and he was reacting on impulse. I hurriedly dialed the radio frequency to contact my squadron's supervisor of flying who controlled the flying operations from the ground. After calling, I arranged my formation and raced back to the base. The formation was split all over the airspace, so rather than spend precious time getting everyone back together, I directed we go back in flights of two jets. But there was another problem. We all had too much fuel to be able to land. Rather than dump the fuel overboard, which would take upwards of six to nine minutes, we got together in twos and did some basic fighter maneuvering. These maneuvers are done in full afterburner, and with a fuel burn rate sometimes in excess of 100,000 pounds per hour, it was the most expeditious way to get to landing weight. As we all requested clearance to fly out of the airspace back to Otis, the radios were crowded with communications. I said, "It sounds like we are at war."

That was the trigger. Everything changed in an instant. The confusion, the chaos, and uncertainty, combined with the rapidly changing external environment, added up to a "high-pressure situation," at least in reference to my worldview.

I contacted the supervisor of flying (SOF) again and asked for an update. In the air, we still had no idea what was going on. The situation was so dynamic that the SOF didn't have anything concrete to say except, "After you land, stay at your jets; we'll run the classified packs out to you." He was referring to the classified codes and guidance we flew with on alert. The "smart packs" neatly fit into the leg pocket in our g-suits and were required to be alert status. In light of recent events, it seemed we had been drafted for alert duty.

I said to myself, "Yeh, right, I'll stay by my jet." I knew the process to post-flight and refuel my Eagle was typically two hours, so I figured I had time to go into the squadron and see what exactly was happening.

I quickly taxied to my parking spot and could see maintenance personnel scurrying around the flight line. On the edge of the ramp, I saw that racks of live missiles had emerged from their hardened storage facilities. With the exception of positioning live weapons outside the alert facility, I had never seen that at Otis before. I grabbed my gear, signed the forms, and ran into the squadron. Most of the squadron personnel were huddled by the small television in the break room. United Airlines Flight 175 had just hit the World Trade Center. Dismayed, one of the Life Support Technicians turned to me and said, "It's a goddamn Tom Clancy novel!" It was obvious now that we were at war.

For some reason, all I could think about was the trip I had leaving Chicago with United Airlines the next day. As fate would have it, I was also a First Officer at UAL and was to pilot a 737 from Chicago to the west coast somewhere. Fully clad in my flying gear, I tried in vain to call the crew desk at United to let them know I would not make the departure time the next day. When I had no luck, I called home. My wife answered and I cut her off, "Listen, I don't know what's going on, but I am going flying. I am okay, but please call United and tell them I won't make my trip tomorrow."

All she could say was, "Be careful."

In a high-pressure situation, it is easy to misprioritize. It was nice she was watching out for me, or "Checking my 6."

A call came over the intercom in the squadron beckoning Bob "Bam Bam" Martyn and me to the Operations Desk. I flashed around the corner and passed a coworker who was crying.

She said, "My brother works at the World Trade Center!" I tossed her my cell phone and said, "Call him," and then I ran down the hall.

At the Operations Desk, I could see several pilots working on a 24-hour manning plan, and another was on the phone with maintenance to plan how they would generate, or prepare, the full squadron of jets. The previously dormant jets would have to be fueled, loaded with weapons, and accepted by a qualified pilot before they could fly. Two more pilots ran to the Command Post to read the new tasking coming in.

"Bam Bam, Opus, Doogie, and Rosey, you will be in the first four jets. Two will be ready in 15 minutes and two more in 30," Tracer said.

I looked at Tracer, the commander, and thought, "I can't believe it." It was the quickest jet maintenance turnaround I had ever heard of.

Just then, I heard someone say, "Two are ready," followed immediately by another announcement on the intercom by the Command Post to "SCRAMBLE TWO! SCRAMBLE TWO!" Later, someone told me the scramble horn was blasting, but I never heard it. I simply was too focused and was on my own VECTOR.

When I arrived at my jet, a weapons specialist, Matt Jackson, was loading the second of two AIM-9 heat-seeking missiles. The crew chief, Dennis Mills, said, "Opus, it's fueled, has a hot gun with bullets, and Matt is loading another AIM-9."

The term "hot gun" referred to the fact that the 20mm gun was loaded and armed for use.

I had an overwhelming urge to get airborne. It was overpowering. I felt out of control in this high-pressure situation and I wanted to exact an infinitesimal amount of authority by getting airborne. Matt swiftly maneuvered the jammer, the motorized vehicle used to lift missiles into place, with the precision of the Thunderbirds. I yelled toward Matt, "Get that thing out of the way; I'm going with one." Then I turned to Dennis, "When I taxi out, if there is any panel open or anything wrong with the jet, stop me, fix it, and get out of the way." Of course, there was nothing wrong with the jet. Dennis was too good to have missed anything.

Our top-notch intelligence specialist, Joe Kelleher, arrived, appeared out of nowhere, breathless, "There are up to eight airliners airborne with bombs on board. We know of an American jet out of Dulles and a United jet. I think you are going after the United jet. They are turning jets away from Europe and the rumor is some have crashed because they've run out of fuel. IT'S FRIGGIN' CHAOS; good luck, dude!" We were finding out real-time what the actual air picture was, and the information was not accurate. It reminded me of an old fighter pilot adage: *Lose Sight, Lose Fight.*

The United jet to which Joe referred turned out to be United Airlines Flight 93, which was a Boeing 757-200 that flew the Newark, New Jersey to San Francisco route. On board that day were only 38 passengers and seven crew members, which was an unusually low load factor for that flight. UAL 93 took off at 8:42 a.m., approximately 40 minutes late. At 9:28 a.m., the pilots Captain Jason Dahl and First Officer LeRoy Homer checked in with Cleveland Center en route, reporting their altitude and adding a report of "light chop," meaning they had encountered a small amount of turbulent air. About a minute later, the one of the pilots was heard screaming frantically, "Get out of here!!"

United Airlines dispatchers, whose job is to aid the Captain by providing everything from weight and balance data to weather updates, transmitted a text message over the in-flight data system shortly before the attack. UAL 93 pilots read the ominous message on the screen, "Beware any cockpit intrusion—two a/c hit World Trade Center." Little did they know within minutes they'd be fighting for their lives.

On board, the attack to seize the aircraft began at 9:28:17. A frantic Mayday transmission on the Cleveland Center frequency was met with confusion. Controllers at Cleveland Center nervously repeated their calls to UAL 93 in an attempt to determine the hijackers' intentions. The calls floated anonymously into the ether. By 9:31:57, the hijackers were in control of the jet and the passengers' fate was sealed. At 9:32, one of the terrorists made a call for the passengers to "keep remaining sitting; we have a bomb on board." The rocker switch on a 757 is used by the pilot to communicate to outside agencies and to the passengers and crew on board. It has two positions. One is used to communicate with the controlling agency over the radio and one announces within the plane over the intercom. The hijacker was using the wrong switch.

The jet then climbed from its assigned 35,000 feet to 41,000 feet and began a slow turn to the east. It was clear my colleagues at United were no longer in control of the jet. Controllers on the ground realized that the plane had been hijacked. When the transponder was switched off at 9:41, action had to be taken. The transponder is an on-board system that indicates the aircraft's position and altitude to the ground controllers through a unique code put in to the system by the pilots. There is a special code inserted by pilots during a hijacking to surreptitiously inform authorities the plane has been commandeered. Obviously, the terrorists knew this and turned the system off to confuse and mask their intentions.

At the time, we had no idea where this rogue flight was headed. Command authorities speculated that its target was either New York or Washington, D.C., with the most probable target being the U.S. capital. In either case, the risk level was so high that they could not take a chance. My pair of two Eagles were to approach from the east while two F-16s approached from the west. Duff and Nasty were already over New York and two F-16s were over Washington, providing a last-chance "goalie cap" over the nation's capital.

Passengers were moved to the rear of the aircraft. There, they began to make calls to loved ones, a postscript to their tragic story. After realizing the hijacking was a suicide mission, they decided to act.

At the same time back at Otis, I quickly wrote down some notes and scampered up the ladder. I started to taxi to the runway and saw Bam Bam just pulling out of the chocks a few parking spots to my left. I followed Bam Bam to the runway and checked my flight controls and engines, and armed my ejection seat. We rolled on to runway 5 at Otis and Bam Bam quickly accelerated into the distance. I pushed up my throttles, checked the power at 80% on both engines and, with everything indicating normal, after 15 seconds I selected afterburner. I was pushed back in my seat as I sped off. At 120 knots, I slowly pulled the stick back and felt the nose gently rise to the air. I retracted the landing gear after being SCRAMBLED, cleared the end of runway 5 and kept the engines in afterburner to trade some fuel for the most speed I could gather while climbing to altitude. I wanted to get to my target quickly, but at the same time, I wanted an eternity to pass so that the situation could resolve itself. I glanced to the left and saw a white van pass impotently on the road underneath me. The sound of air whooshed over the canopy and the jet shook with eagerness as I gained speed. My F-15 felt like a dog waiting for his master to throw his favorite tennis ball to be fetched. A man with a beard was driving south on Route 130 out of Sandwich toward the town of Mashpee and was straining to watch me over his steering wheel. I could tell by his expression that he was following the attacks on his radio. Life was in slow motion. I checked that the gear was up and locked, set my radar, checked my engines, and then just listened. Meanwhile, I had a second to think. The stream of consciousness going through my mind played the same tape over and over: "I don't want to do this; I don't want to do this." I had never been so scared.

Duff and Nasty were over New York City. In the bending of time that permeated the event, I'd lost track of their position; in fact, I had forgotten they had even been SCRAMBLED. Still, I remembered a story that Duff told of his first mission in Operation Desert Storm. Upon hearing of the impending commencement of the war that night in 1991, his squadron commander asked his pilots if they were scared. Of course, no one admitted it, but they all were. His counsel vividly came back to me as Cape Cod faded beneath my jet, "Scared is okay, scared will keep you alive; just don't let it get in the way of you doing your job." It was time for me to focus and do my job.

I was in a squadron with the best trained fighter pilots in the world. I had flown in combat many times, but my wingmen and I never imagined that we'd have to turn the deadly power of the F-15 Eagle on citizens of our own country in the name of their own defense. Further complicating the issue was the fact that I was a pilot with United Airlines. I wondered if I had flown with anyone aboard Flight 93. I wondered if anyone I knew had died in the crashes at the World Trade Center. Worst of all, I wondered if any of my squadron mates, my brothers, were on those flights. The implications were too colossal to comprehend. It was too much to process and it wasn't the time. The massive consequences were paralyzing and this was a time to focus and act. I turned to the north and could see the beautiful skyline of Boston as the tip of the Cape passed silently, innocently below me.

Even though UAL 93 was known to be hostile, there were other, more pressing issues to sort out amid the confusion. NEADS VECTORed my formation to its first target, "Panta 1, target is bearing 040 for 42 miles." I acknowledged and we turned to the north-northeast for cutoff. NEADS did not have radio contact with the civilian controlling agency, Boston Center, so we coordinated our direction to deconflict with other air traffic. It was total chaos. The aircraft in question had not checked in with Boston Center as expected, and therefore, was under suspicion. We'd let UAL 93 come to us, so it could wait. Our only option was to consider anything moving in the air to be suspicious. I locked my radar to the target and called it out to my flight lead, Bam Bam Martyn.

"Panta 2, target BRA 037/38, 17000." I was telling Bam Bam that the target was 38 miles northeast of us at 17,000 feet. We reselected full afterburner and went supersonic. Our path would have us intercept the target just east of Logan International Airport. As the range closed, we gained a visual with the target and could see it was a C-130, a military transport aircraft. I immediately threw my throttles to idle anticipating the immense overtake I had built up and slid forward in my seat. A C-130 cruises at a considerably lower airspeed than an F-15. Bam Bam controlled his closure with a different technique. As we approached the C-130, he pulled up and over it, completing a perfect barrel roll and ending up on its right wing. It was breathtaking. I took up position on the C-130's left wing. The pilot sitting in the left seat of the C-130 was unaware that the world below was on fire. He was unaware that two, fully-loaded F-15 jets were poised to take lethal action not three feet away from where he was enjoying his boxed lunch. Maybe the relative movement of my jet caught his attention, or maybe he wanted a glimpse of Beantown, but either way, when he turned to look to the left his eyes opened as wide as the Grand Canyon. We rocked our wings to signify he was "intercepted," and he acknowledged by rocking back. His panicky voice called out on the universal emergency radio frequency known as "guard."

"F15's intercepting the C-130 over Boston, state intentions."

Bam Bam retorted curtly, "Contact Boston Center immediately," and we were off. It was amazing to me that in the beginning moments of the most important mission of my life, our formation was SCRAMBLED to intercept a United States military C-130. Even though things were changing, in the Air Defense game, things remained the same. The mistake would be debriefed at a later date. I thought back to the intercept of the Coast Guard jet and the U.S. Navy Destroyer. It did; however, foreshadow the day's ensuing events.

Dennis "Doogie" Doonan and Joe "Rosey" McGrady were Panta 3 and 4. They rejoined us sometime shortly after takeoff, but there was so much going on so quickly that I didn't even know they were a mile in trail until NEADS called them. While we assessed the C-130, they were told by NEADS to proceed east off the coast and intercept a KC-10 Air Refueling jet that was in a package with six A-10 aircraft on their way back from Europe. A fighter jet does not have the range to make it back from Europe without this "gas station in the sky," and these were common flights between the continents. The plan was to commandeer the KC-10, have the A-10s land somewhere short of their destination, and use the fuel on board the tanker for our current operation.

Doogie tried in vain to reach the tanker on the radio. He pulled up beside them and, after a few moments of confusion, contacted them on guard. "KC-10 at east of Boston with six A-10s and two F-15s on your wing, say your call sign."

"This is Gold 69," emerged from the massive hunk of flying metal.

In my mind's eye, I was taken back to a time when I was flying across the Mediterranean Sea from Germany to Saudi Arabia. We were on a ferry mission taking 18 F-15s to replace a squadron at Al Karj Air Base for Operation Southern Watch. Out of nowhere, a U.S. Navy F-14 Tomcat showed up behind the tanker and sat in position as if to say, "Can I have some gas?" Normally, this would have been an Eagle pilot's dream and a ferocious dog fight would ensue! But this day we were on a ferry mission. It was a matter of national security that all of our F-15s arrive in country ready to go. This was a point-A-to-point-B mission and nothing else. Discipline dictated focus. Needless to say we needed every drop of gas, so the F-14 was scoffed and he went on his way. It's amazing what invades and interrupts your train of thought during a high pressure situation.

"Gold 69, this is Panta 3; we need you to come with us for a current mission and tell the flight of A-10s to land at Barnes Air National Guard Base." He gave the bearing and range to Barnes.

The confused tanker pilot asked, "What's going on?"

In classic "Doogie" style, he said, "Some serious shit." Gold 69 was parked over Boston to service Panta 3 and 4 for the next six hours without protest.

Back on board United 93, anxious passengers schemed. They knew the hijackers intended to kill everyone with another suicide attack. As they devised a plan of action, the killers fumbled at the controls. At 9:57:55, passengers stormed the cockpit after a courageous Todd Beamer yelled, "Let's Roll!"

The passengers of United 93 became the first and most unlikely warriors in the war on terrorism. The hijackers retreated and cowered in the cockpit and realized their mission was foiled. At 10:02:23, they rolled the plane and pointed it to the Earth. Unbeknownst to us, less than 50 seconds later it impacted in Shanksville, Pennsylvania.[1]

Suddenly, a report came via the FAA that a large civilian airliner was seen flying low and fast near Martha's Vineyard. The Vineyard was about 50 miles south and we pushed up the engines to exceed the mach again. Our radars swept low and we inspected all of the traffic in the vicinity of the Vineyard, but we

---

[1] National Public Radio, "Timeline for United Airlines Flight 93: Controllers Struggle with Decision to Shoot Down Plane," October 23, 2008. Retrieved from http://www.npr.org/templates/story/story.php?storyId=1962910. This page also has audio clips of the actual radio transmissions. There is one entry in this story with which I disagree. It mentions "discussions" about military assistance with Flight 93, but it says no one from the FAA requested specific military intervention. While in fact this may be true, I know that I was aware of Flight 93 and in a larger sense, whether directed or implied, any rogue airliner (after the first two impacted WTC 1 and 2) would have been dispatched before finding its target in my opinion. Obviously, my perspective on the day's events is also sourced.

saw nothing suspicious. Bam Bam descended, speaking with Boston Center and Cape Approach for the appropriate clearance for deconfliction. Meanwhile, his radios were barely readable and very scratchy. I stayed up around 10,000 feet and relayed radio communication to Bam Bam while also working with NEADS to keep a mental track of the remaining civil traffic while the FAA sorted out UAL 93's status. It was a very clear day so it was easy to maintain visual contact with him, even though I was almost two miles above him. As Bam Bam swept the south side of Martha's Vineyard, it was obvious that the report of a large airliner flying low near the island was false. He pulled his nose up and we rejoined, heading southwest. He recycled his radios from on to off then back on again and was back to full strength. We could see smoke in the distance. A dim, eerie, silent trail of dull brown slinked its way sheepishly up the north side of Long Island. It pointed to utter despair. At its end, two of the most brilliant engineering feats constructed by man struggled in vain to stand long enough for their occupants to vacate. I took a moment to curse the terrorists who perpetrated the attack, said a small prayer, and then focused back on the business at hand, still disbelieving what was apparent.

"Panta 1, this is Huntress, standby for words on your target." Huntress was the name assigned to NEADS for all radio communication. They continued, "Panta 1, skip it, skip it, target is faded, standby." United Airlines Flight 93 from Newark to San Francisco was down.

"Panta 1, copy, skip it, authenticate Charlie, Charlie, Romeo."

"Huntress authenticates, "November."

NEADS was instructing us to disregard UAL 93 because the radar track had been lost. We would find out hours later that the flight had crashed and some of the first heroes of the War on Terror had made the ultimate sacrifice to thwart another inconceivable attack. Because the communication was so bizarre that day, we decided to "authenticate" the order to "skip it." I never thought I'd have to authenticate an order over the skies of America like I had to over the skies of Iraq, but then again, I had never imagined a day like September 11, 2001.

For a small moment in time, we did not have air superiority over our sovereign skies—an unbelievable thought. Still, the response being correct, we awaited orders and flew southwest towards the smoke, climbing and conserving fuel.

"Panta 1, Huntress, continue southwest and set up a combat air patrol over bull's-eye." Duff, the mission commander, declared bull's-eye, the reference point from which all positional reporting originated, as the rubble that had been the World Trade Center and we proceeded to the smoke to join our squadron mates.

We checked in with New York Center, but there was no answer. Huntress instructed us to check in with New York Approach instead and gave us the frequency. The air picture was so convoluted that the Air Route Traffic Control Centers (ARTCC) had basically relinquished control. Their job normally was to guide air traffic in the high-altitude structure to ensure safe operations. The FAA was in the process of instructing every single civilian airliner airborne in the United States to land at the closest suitable airport.

We knew there was a procedure to expedite this seemingly insurmountable task. The FAA pulled the plan know as SCATANA (Security Control of Air Traffic and Navigation Aids) from some forgotten shelf, brushed the vintage-1958 dust off the cover, and implemented the plan. It sanctioned the federal government to assume full control of all domestic air traffic and the navigational aids they utilized in the event of an emergency. In the 1950s, it was devised to clear the air picture so that a long-range attack by Soviet bombers could be defended against. SCATANA had never before been implemented, but it proved the adage that even a mediocre plan executed well is better than no plan at all. Within two hours, all civil air traffic, with the exception of some helicopters working rescue operations, were on the ground.

Working with New York Approach Control meant that our FAA "eyes" spanned about 25 miles around JFK, LaGuardia, and Newark airports. Of course, our radar could see much further, but our seemingly unmanageable challenge was to try to understand the motivation of each "target." I had just witnessed three aircraft turned into missiles. Were there more out there?

Radio time was at a premium. Duffy and Nash had split and were furiously tracking down hundreds of flights in the crowded New York airspace.

"Panta 45, Panta 1 is on station at 15,000 feet," Bam Bam broadcasted to Duff. I flew in tactical formation with Bam Bam.

"Panta 1, orbit over bull's-eye and standby," Duffy said, in a matter-of-fact tone.

It was comforting to hear the familiar voices and they reminded me of another old fighter pilot adage: *Check Six.* I don't know whether it was true or not, but Duff and Nasty sounded confident and in control. All I knew was that between the four of us, we were confident that our capability and experience could bring down many other country's entire air forces. In the absence of guidance, Duffy was running the air war. In vintage, fighter-pilot fashion, he had taken control of the situation while those on the ground struggled with how to proceed. We had never been in a situation like this before, so with a lack of guidance, it was up to us to act. Hours earlier, I had been on a practice Defensive Counter Air (DCA) mission. The construct of that mission seemed to be appropriate for the current operation. We had no idea how many airliners were hijacked, what their intended targets were, their altitude, or their intentions. We did not know the axis or method of attack. These factors are all critical to planning our maneuvers during a DCA mission, but instead, we had no information. We did know that we had to protect the city of New York. That was our mission objective and the risk level was high.

Duff decided to set up a point defense around the city, just as in the DCA scenario I had set up for training hours before. Ground zero was our reference point and the targets in the area were called out in reference to it. The tanker was positioned at 20,000 overhead. Since we were flying in a void of actionable information, we decided that the most effective way to win this battle was to let the enemy come to us. In this manner, we could protect the city, preserve the resources we had (fuel and weapons), and control the fight. Simply put, making a good decision is based, in part, on the luxury of having good information, and on 9/11, our insatiable appetite for information was starved—there was none to be had. Until an airliner "tripped" the commit criteria, we had to disregard it. This way, we could not be decoyed out of our area of responsibility, thereby opening the door for another target to sneak in.

As I looked over my shoulder, now about 500 feet over LaGuardia Airport heading northwest, I saw Manhattan enveloped in a cloud of dust and smoke. It was surreal to be flying over New York City at 500 feet above the crowded roofscapes.[2] I turned to the south and flew down the Hudson towards ground zero. The second tower had just capitulated. I was horrified. I could see a few tops of buildings uncomfortably peeking through the carnage at the sky gasping for air. That was the trigger. Again, everything changed in an instant.

I was not sure how we would allay these cowardly attacks on our country, but I was sure I was going to make them stop—and stop right now. All at once, as if the entire universe was rushing into my body at the speed of light, I concentrated like I had never concentrated before. In a moment of pure

---

[2] One personal note: Weeks later I met up with a fellow United Airlines pilot and great guy, Oscar Sanchez. He was the first Captain I flew with when I started at United Airlines and he went way above and beyond the call of duty to help me understand how to be an airline pilot. I saw him months after the tragedy and we shared stories about September 11, 2001. While I was flying over NYC that day, he was enjoying some coffee on his balcony having just moved back to the City. Just then, an F-15 screamed over him, afterburners blazing. He knew something was very wrong. We looked at each other in silence for a minute and I said, "1 in 4 chance it was me."

clarity, I said a prayer for those who had fallen. I could almost see their souls, reluctantly yet inevitably, floating away from the pandemonium of the attack, searching peacefully for what was to follow. I prayed for strength. Fear and apprehension vanished. In that moment, I was jerked back to reality by the frantic shrieks on the radio. It was time to focus, and focus I did with a precision like I had never had before. When the second World Trade Tower succumbed, I this attack had to stop.

*   *   *

When I reflect on September 11, 2001, I am reminded of a quote I once read by Oliver Wendell Holmes:

> **_"A great man represents a strategic point in the campaign of history, and part of his greatness consists of his being there."_**

I certainly lay no claim to the superlative "great." I was simply "there" on September 11. Being there and functioning well in the morass of that day was a testament to the training, development, and most importantly, the preparation that I had assiduously pursued in my leadership experience. It could have been any other pilot in my squadron that day and they would have executed flawlessly. On 9/11, as Holmes says, I was "there."

*   *   *

How do you feel in a high-pressure situation? When I am working with some of the country's best and brightest corporate leaders, they speak of feeling like I did on 9/11. They feel out of sorts, uncomfortable, uncertain, afraid, and unsure, among other things. Most of all, they feel SCRAMBLED. Normal processes are interrupted, simple things become difficult, the standard flow of action becomes disjointed—everything is SCRAMBLED. Perception, direction, purpose, and confidence are SCRAMBLED.

Over the past twenty years, I have used the principles that enabled me to lead and succeed under pressure in combat to excel in my business career. In my survey of literature, I gaze over the prolific market for leadership books. The sheer volume of work in this enterprise implies a vast readership with an insatiable appetite for techniques to become a better leader. Further, it implies that the topic of leadership is itself unwieldy for many readers. If one could read a book and be a great leader, the world would be filled with George Washington's and Winston Churchill's. I offer this book, therefore, with a more focused purpose so that it can help you produce tangible results.

This book is about
LEADERSHIP in HIGH-PRESSURE SITUATIONS.

Preparing for tremendously dynamic combat situations easily translates to the business world because the fog that clouds decision making and execution in combat has the same effect in business. Specifically, this book is not meant as an esoteric look at leadership as a behavior or action. I've decided to leave that discussion to the professors nestled in the comfort of their ivory towers who are not accountable for producing results. Rather, this book is focused like a laser beam on how the lessons I have learned about leadership in my combat and business experience will show you how to lead and succeed in high-pressure situations. In my business experience, I have found that the leaders who can execute in the foreboding, uncertain and murky environment of high-pressure situations are the leaders that produce results consistently in any situation.

In combat, my squadron mates and I bet our lives on the efficacy of these principles of *high-pressure leadership* and in business I bet my livelihood on them. The good news is that I am still alive and business is prospering! A good place to start is by defining what "pressure" is in your world. Leading in the benign environment of predictable schedules, superstar team players, and a clear business landscape is simple. But, if you spend at least part of your day "putting out fires," dealing with dynamic personalities, or responding to relentlessly shifting internal and external environments, you will get something from this book. Pressure as a concept is amorphous. It manifests itself surreptitiously at times and with the full force of a tsunami at others. September 11, 2001 was a tsunami. Other high-pressure situations slither to life over the span of days, weeks, or even years to become manifest in tension-filled episodes.

The world is living an example of this right now with the global financial crisis, the underpinnings of which began some 30 years ago. In 1977, the U.S. Congress passed the Community Reinvestment Act, which relaxed credit requirements to borrow money. More recently, regulators compelled banks to carry the resultant "subprime mortgages" on their books as "marked to market." This is when a security, in this case the mortgage, is re-priced daily at the end of trading to reflect the market's closing value of the security itself. Add to this the years of historically low interest rates allowing more people to borrow more and more money, which produced an excessive money supply and effectively inflated the real estate market. The market responded and rose to an unsustainable level. Finally, in 1999, the Glass-Steagal Act, which segregated investment banks from commercial banks, expired. With the separation between the two gone, banks leveraged themselves at a rate of up to 40:1. So, for every $1 they physically "had," they borrowed $40. Covertly, the amalgamation of these ingredients led to a high-pressure situation that no one was willing to admit had been there to see for years and years.[3]

No matter the situation or how noticeably it is manifest, the bottom line is that the perception of pressure is different to each individual. As a leader, you must be aware that your team will perceive different levels of pressure in different ways. I remember preparing for a combat mission that I flew over Northern Iraq in support of Operation Northern Watch to enforce the United Nations mandated no-fly zone. It was 1997 and I was based at Incirlik Air Base in Turkey. I had flown over Iraq many times in the years before and I understood the flow of a typical mission. The mission was simple: show a presence. Still, a real fighter pilot understands that whenever you are over hostile territory, your full, undivided, unrelenting attention is demanded. That day, I was leading a brand new mission-qualified pilot on his first sortie over Iraq. He was a rising star with great potential. He soared through pilot training and F-15 training, winning just about every award they had invented. His qualifications were impeccable and soon he would graduate from being a wingman to becoming a flight lead—a very important step in a new pilot's development.

We began the day with a run by the chow hall to get some breakfast and I noticed he was quieter than usual. I knew why. It was his first mission, and he was nervous. When we arrived at the squadron, his anxiety was palpable. I began to brief our mission in preparation for the big mission briefing that would occur about 30 minutes later. I took a little extra time to go over the procedures in great detail, hoping that the depth of the briefing would help to ally some of his apprehension. It didn't work! The one thing we had going in our favor was that

---

[3] I am neither an economist nor am I an analyst, but since most "experts" missed the warning signs of a crash for years, I figured my examination of the economics is just as valid in as much as all those we depended upon to warn us of the impending doom were asleep at the wheel. Nonetheless, the net result is that we are now all in a high-pressure situation. Credit also goes to Vaughn "El J" Littlejohn of the Zulu Capital Group for helping in my interpretation of these events.

Operation Northern Watch missions were, by design, benign sorties. The political ramifications of losing a United States plane over Iraq in 1997 were prohibitive. The risk level was too high, so we carefully planned to avoid problem areas yet still achieve our objective of enforcing the no-fly zone to show our presence.

My wingman was nervous from wheels up to touchdown. That was fine. Predictably, our perceptions of pressure were completely different. These factors filtered our view of the mission, from the planning to the debriefing phases. First, experience: I had done it before; he hadn't. Second, skill set: I had more qualifications and flying hours; he was new. Third, preparation: I studied the mission the day before ad nauseam; he played tennis the night before. These are but a few reasons, and even though I was under pressure, the level of perceived pressure was far less for me than my wingman.

Perception of pressure depends on an individual's worldview, skill set, and attitude. This is part of the reason that adding pressure to any situation disrupts an individual's flow, as well as the team's. When I consult with a corporate team regarding challenges they face, I will stop them and ask periodically, "Are we in a high-pressure situation?" Typically, the split will be 60% no answers and 40% yes answers— IRRESPECTIVE OF THE SITUATION! It all comes down to perception, but with high-pressure situations, perception is reality. Or is it?

The *American Heritage Dictionary* defines "perception" as *the recognition and interpretation of sensory stimuli based chiefly on memory.*[4] The interesting part of this definition to me is that "based chiefly on memory" statement. One key to leadership in a high-pressure situation is shifting the perceived circumstances, and more importantly, the response to these perceived circumstances, from the unconscious to the

---

[4] The American Heritage Dictionary of the English Language, 4th Edition. Boston: Houghton Mifflin Company, 2006.

conscious. This empowers leaders to, as my dear friend and mentor Sam Samsel of the Samsel Consulting Group says, "act on purpose."[5] Acting "on purpose" rather than reacting is vitally important in a high-pressure situation. In order to act on purpose, leaders must communicate a tactical plan to execute. The plan I have taught all over the United States can provide you with the framework to confidently handle whatever challenges are presented and not only to act on purpose, but also to thrive!

As we consider the special conditions associated with leadership in high-pressure situations, it is important to understand what a high-pressure situation is and how it can be identified. Most of my clients are tactically oriented. They are "do-ers," but taking time to consider high-pressure situations strategically will allow you to shift your response from an unconscious reaction to a conscious, purposeful process response, which is a critical step in being a leader in a high-pressure environment. Once you understand how to identify the situation, you can position yourself for success by anticipating how the individuals and teams around you tend to react under these conditions. In so doing, you mitigate the effect of surprise and emotion, or help cut through the fog and friction associated with stress, so that you can get to work overcoming the challenge presented. This approach helps form the foundational basis for my methodology to thrive—the high-performance culture. From there, I will show you how to overlay my simple yet effective line of attack: the ACE Methodology. This plan helps teams all over the country make the vitally important shift from reaction to action—three simple steps that anyone can use in the critical period that follows the recognition of a high-pressure situation. The goal is to handle stressful situations in stride. The key to doing that is preparation. Once the situation is

---

[5] Sam Samsel is the Principle and Owner of The Samsel Group, a Boston-based consulting company. He is my mentor and my friend. His distinguished resume is too large to fit here, but includes being on the Board of American Express and being a prolific philanthropist. Every time I meet with Sam, I feel like I am defending a doctoral dissertation!

recognized, understood, and handled, you will see that you have created an opportunity upon which to capitalize. From a business perspective, the inability to make the most of these opportunities is where companies leave money on the table, and that is where my unique time-sensitive planning tool called VECTOR fills the void. Once we have the process and tools to lead and succeed under pressure, it is valuable to take a look at leadership as a skill set with our newfound perspective.

This book is about leadership under pressure. Just as I found in the skies above New York on September 11, 2001, the concepts are simple, though they're not quite as easy to put into practice. So where do we start? We start at the beginning. For fighter pilots, we have the luxury of drawing from decades of those who preceded us with their own brand of raunchy wisdom, no-nonsense perspective, and understated simplicity. This tradition is not only the foundation for a fighter pilot, but it is also the standard and responsibility a pilot inherits when strapping on a multi-million-dollar high-performance fighter jet. It starts simply with what I call the "Three Axioms of a Fighter Pilot"—three little crutches that are universally applicable to any high pressure situation in business, combat, or life.

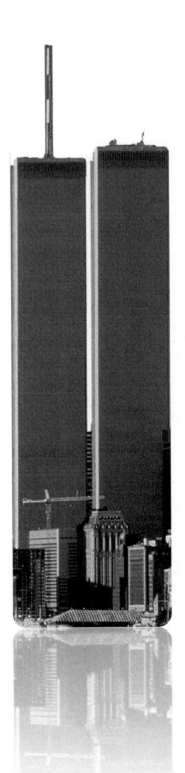

We Shall Never Forget.

2

The Mindset:
Three Axioms to Live By

"What are you doing today to become the best version of yourself?"

—Matthew Kelly

II. The Mindset: Three Axioms to Live By

Five hundred feet below me was the city of New York. I darted around the city chasing down airliners, helicopters, and anything else in the air. The second tower had just collapsed. Debris, smoke, and dreams from ground zero drifted northeast. I swung up from Manhattan to fly up the Hudson on the east side of the river, where I took a second to look around. I will never forget seeing the roads going out of the city as being a complete log jam. Nothing was moving and people were abandoning their cars. The roads going into the city were completely clear, so people jumped the barrier dividing the road and decided to walk northward out of the carnage. I thought, "Where are they going?"

The answer was obvious: they were going somewhere other than the new, albeit temporary, epicenter of terrorism. An amazing change in culture was happening below me. Mutual support abounded. People offered water to those who were thirsty, others helped guide those in shock, and still others lent support to first responders. People came together. All over the city, people were leading under pressure.

The enormity of the day was still finding its way through the city. My mission was clear, make sure everything in the air was visually identified, intercepted and guided to land at the closest airfield. I flew low and fast over Central Park southbound toward the Empire State Building. I looked down to see a person jogging on the path, oblivious to the events unfolding. At first I scowled, thinking, "How could someone go for a run at a time like this?" But then I realized, like most in the country, our eyes were just being opened to a new reality. I banked left and watched the middle floors of the Empire State Building pass to the right of me. I banked back to the right around the building and headed south to ground zero, my cranium on a swivel looking for air traffic in the area.[6] Across the Hudson just east of Newark International Airport, a large formation of helicopters were marshalling over a fuel tank farm. Three helicopters were line abreast, with another two sets of three about a half-mile behind them. It reminded me of marshalling in the Honus Military Operating Area in Saudi Arabia, waiting for the "vul time" or vulnerability period, for our push into Iraq for Operation Southern Watch to click off. They waited, orderly, for their call into the city to rescue survivors, but unfortunately they were not needed.

Above me there was nothing. The clear blue sky had been previously crowded by airliner contrails, which were now dissipating. The white tubular clouds written across the deep blue were slowly fading to transparency. Nothing was flying. Nothing. It was a sight I, like most modern Americans, had never seen before. That was the trigger. I knew our lives had changed forever.

*　　　*　　　*

I flew high performance jets for almost twenty years. Our culture was predominately made up of "type A" personalities, competitive, over achievers. In such a culture, excellence is

---

[6] Sometimes in a military operation, you want to execute under complete secrecy and sometimes your objective lends itself to being as overt as you possibly can. On September 11, 2001, for the attackers and for the citizens of the country alike, it was paramount that all knew that we were in the air to regain air superiority and air supremacy over the skies of the country. I wanted the people of New York to see and hear me so they'd know that we were on scene. It took me five years to understand how important this had been. I found that I could not watch any news coverage whatsoever about 9/11 after the event. I remember going to a speaking engagement on the four-year anniversary in Boston, when an early morning radio show played the FAA tapes of Flight 93 being hijacked. I got so sick to my stomach that I had to pull off Route 495 North and compose myself. On 9/11/2006, I finally watched as Fox News and others replayed the coverage from 2001 in real time. I was amazed as I watched Mayor Rudy Giuliani leaving his ad hoc Command Post and walking with his staff through the streets of Manhattan. A loud jet screamed over their position and one staffer yelled, "There are more coming!" Rudy calmly looked skyward and said, "They're ours." I can't tell you how much pride I have when I tell that story.

demanded and is expected. We use this energy to push ourselves "to the edge of the envelope" in the same way we push our flying machines. As my wife has to remind me, I am just a man! She also reminds me that I make mistakes. When I make mistakes, I always try to learn from them, just as I did in every mission debrief I have been a part of. It was the driver for constant improvement and it worked so well that the United States Air Force was one critical part of the best fighting force in the world.

Our high-performance culture is steeped in tradition. The continuous line dates back to the earliest days of aviation. We draw on this stream of consciousness on a visceral level and feel a connection with those who wrote the book on flying so many years ago. Their legacy is our foundation. Our pact is to continue pushing the edge of the envelope out and redefine its limitations. In doing so, we form the basis of a high-performance culture.

Demanding a high-performance culture accelerates personal and professional development. It also compels us to reach as far as we can in order to challenge ourselves and each other towards excellence. Picture yourself on the phone speaking with a high-level executive from one of your suppliers. You are "in the zone" and are in delicate negotiations to build a lasting, profitable relationship. Suddenly, your concentration is shattered when one of your team members knocks on your door. She has *another* question about the task you delegated to her last week. Now let's stipulate that you took all of the preparatory steps to enable her to succeed in this tasking. Among other things you:

→ Set a clear, definable, quantifiable and attainable goal;
→ Provided her the necessary resources;
→ Identified an aggressive yet reasonable timeline.

When a team member has been given a task and all of the tools to succeed, yet still seems timid about running at supersonic speed to complete it, it may be time for a different approach.

There are many reasons that you delegate tasks in the workplace. They can range from needing to free up time for more important functions, to mentoring subordinates into leadership positions. Still, the act of delegation does not in and of itself assure that your team member will take the ball and run. In these cases, a new and innovative way to supercharge productivity may be the answer. Inspire your team members to be leaders, no matter how small or mundane the task. This method will encourage your team to embrace their assignment, will empower them to "own" the process, will build a culture of leaders in your workplace, and will transform the prevailing mindset, attitude, and approach to the task at hand. The effect of working within a high-performance culture of leaders transcends the day-to-day tasking of a job. When I work with teams who are trying to instill the notion of a high-performance culture, I like to start by asking them what their personal definition of success is. The answers run the gamut. Some deal with income, others deal with quality of life, and others deal with status, but they usually all address things related to their professional situation. I conceptualize the idea of success differently. Admittedly, my definition of success has evolved over time with the lessons I have learned along the course of my professional and personal maturation. So, I try to impart to them that their definition needs to be universally applicable to every aspect of their lives. I offer the definition I have of success:[7]

1. Knowing what you want;
2. Finding out how to get it;
3. Getting it;
4. Asking yourself if it was worth getting.

---

[7] I developed these in a mentoring session with Sam Samsel.

Simple and straight forward! The beauty of this definition is that it applies to everything I do. I devote time to planning, briefing, executing, and debriefing, a very important and universally applicable process I have lived by all my adult life. In this way, this definition fits with how "I do business." Take a moment to think strategically and ask yourself to define success in your own life. Does your definition apply to all aspects of your life, and not just your job? Then, debrief yourself. Take the last goal you had and ask yourself: Did I know what I wanted when I started? Did I take the time to prepare to get it? Did I get it? Was it worth it? Why or why not? If I had to bet, I'd say that the debrief you just did was in reference to a business goal you had. Now, debrief yourself on a personal goal unrelated to business. In my experience, this is where the process tends to disengage. We often are comfortable with the processes we work within at our job, but at home we spend most of the time putting out fires. It is hard to be successful when we just jump into a situation, letting our unconscious, learned behavior drive the fight. I have a humorous story to illustrate. During our training on methodology with Fighter Associates, I used to ask several volunteers to step in front of the audience as I hold a Hula-hoop in my hands. I put the ad hoc team of six in a circle and ask them to take hold of the Hula-hoop. Then I tell them that they have one objective: to hold the hoop as a group at shoulder level and lower it to the ground. Of course, I offer the following caveats: they have to rest the hoop on the nails of their thumbs and every member of the team has to touch the hoop at all times. If a thumb loses contact with the hoop, they have to start over. How hard could that be, right? Without fail, the team enthusiastically starts their task. It's easy. After a few seconds, frustration sets in. Someone loses contact with the hoop; people on opposite sides of the hoop have competing ideas on how to complete the task; people in the crowd laugh, creating the perception of pressure—any number of challenges arise to foil their attempts to meet the objective. In all my years of doing this simple simulation exercise, I have had only one team complete the task without help. On the surface, it seems a mystery that only one team would be able to complete the objective; however, when the team debriefs itself, the reason becomes clear. Sometimes when we are presented with a task that seems to be simple, we neglect to devote time to developing even a cursory plan of action for its completion. We instead jump right to the execution phase; after all, how hard could it be? What I find over and over again is that teams who approach seemingly simple tasks with no plan are doomed to fail, or at least to put themselves in a high-pressure fire-fighting situation.

My challenge to you is to move the action from the unconscious to the conscious—the challenge of being a leader. Apply this universal definition of success and follow it up with the process I am going to talk about later on. If you do, you will be amazed how successful you are—and have been!

Fighter pilots are fortunate because our heritage gives us a simple tool to keep focus in the most difficult times. The secret is three universally applicable principles we use to guide us daily. Internalizing these axioms allows us as fighter pilots to cultivate a high-performance culture that maintains a readiness for action. It is not an obvious expression; rather, it tends to be subtle. Still, it is extremely effective. Just as we push our tactical employment to the edge of the envelope, fighter pilots try to push every task to the edge. It harkens back to the World War I pilots passing on the lessons learned from combat to their new protégés to help them live to fly again the next day. Tim Duffy and I also called on these axioms to illustrate the business and leadership principles we brought to our clients. They are:

- ✓ **Speed is Life**
- ✓ **Lose Sight, Lose Fight**
- ✓ **Check Six**

In the early 1900s, these simple "words of wisdom" represented a growing anthology of emerging knowledge being discovered in the skies over the battlefields of World War I. As erudite pilots strapped themselves into their wobbly flying machines and tossed their silk scarves into the wind, combat veterans sent their former students into battle armed with these three axioms and little more. The axioms were meant as a message of survival from the experienced to the new. You see, the book on fighter aviation had just entered chapter one in the early 1900s, and these pilots were the authors. To fill the existing void of information, pilots had only the lessons they had learned in the air, most of which were written in the blood of fallen comrades. The axioms were aimed at saving lives and winning a war. For new pilots on their first combat mission, the message was straightforward: heed these axioms or proceed at your own peril. So, how do these three axioms, born in the infancy of fighter aviation, translate to the contemporary business world? For the answer, let's jump into our vintage World War I Nieuport 28 fighter plane and fly back to the year 1918 into the wild blue skies of Toul, France.

Speed is life. At the beginning of World War I, fighter aircraft crawled onto the scene like an apprehensive infant exploring its ability to move for the first time. They were fragile and unpredictable. Four years later, through the necessity uniquely created in war; they had been transformed into durable fighting machines. Originally, prescient tacticians saw airborne platforms as reconnaissance vehicles to fly over enemy positions, noting formations and movement below. Soon, pilots carried cameras aloft and expanded their scope to detail supply lines and rear operating areas from a perspective previously reserved for flying creatures rather than flying machines. Eventually, a rear position in the aircraft was added for another man whose only job was to take pictures. As reconnaissance planes, both friend and foe, flew impotently past each other on

42

SCRAMBLED – by Martin Richard

the way back and forth to the day's mission, one industrious future fighter pilot decided to bring arms to flight and shot at his adversary, thereby changing the face of war forever. Before long, advances made it possible to mount machine guns synchronized with the propeller; hence, the first fighter airplane was born.

By September 1918, Captain Eddie Rickenbacker had already asserted himself as one of the world's most adroit combat aviators. After being awarded the French Croix de Guerre for downing five German aircraft in one month, Rickenbacker was named the 94th Aero Squadron's Commander. The heralded title of "Fighter ACE" had also been awarded to him for downing enemy planes. Taking to the air with reckless abandon in his Nieuport 28, Rickenbacker soared to altitudes of 17,000 feet at speeds of 120 miles per hour. He was wildly successful. However, it was evident to Rickenbacker that it was impractical to expect similar success from his squadron mates—especially the untested pilots who arrived in theater armed with a lot of attitude, little skill, and no experience. Since there was no real proxy for experience in this extremely stressful venue, Rickenbacker and his peers turned their attention to the machine.

The Nieuport 28 was a hand-me-down airplane given by the French to the inexperienced American pilots. It replaced the obsolete Nieuport 17, which was incapable of matching the performance of the latest German fighters. Notably, advances in armament featuring twin-synchronized machine guns, a more powerful engine, and a completely redesigned wing structure sought to bring parity to fighter aviation. There were still significant limitations. The fuselage was so fine and narrow that the machine guns had to be offset in order to fit. While the French Air Forces employed superior flying machines, the Nieuport filled a desperate hole in production for the Americans. Although it was extremely maneuverable and pilots loved to fly it, its performance was mediocre. There is an old saying in aviation: the best plane in the world is the plane you fly! New American fighter pilots like Alan Winslow and Douglas Campbell, along with Rickenbacker, were flexing muscle in the skies over Europe with their version of the best plane in the world. Technology marched on.

As engineers and designers of the day sought input from their clients, the prevailing thought from the battlefield was that the difference between life and death came down to two things. First, once a pilot had the first few combat missions under his belt, his chances of coming home alive were significantly enhanced. Second, the faster plane wins. Designers could not affect the first so they went to work on the second.

Pilots came to believe that the key to victory was having more speed available than their adversaries. They summed it up succinctly: *Speed is Life.* There was a fine line, though. The relatively fragile airframes could only take so much stress. The challenge would be to design the fastest model possible within the capabilities of the airplane. Speed represented opportunity. Speed permitted pilots to safely exit a fight and return another day if in a position of disadvantage, or to use the speed in order to maneuver their machines to a position of advantage. Speed could make the difference between life and death. Speed could be traded for altitude to zoom above an adversary, allowing the pilot the ability to attack from the high ground, or it could be hoarded and used for lethal slashing attacks to defeat the adversary. Battle to the World War I fighter pilot was a personal, one-on-one event, eye-to-eye and soul-to-soul. Speed was the quintessential element to the pilot because speed was life. Rickenbacker and his mates stirred when the result of their wishes arrived. It was the Spad 8.

The Spad 8 was some 20 miles per hour faster than the Nieuport and could rocket five thousand feet higher. These diminutive differences seemed insignificant to the infantry officer solidly grounded on terra firma gazing with wonder into the sky, but to the World War I fighter pilot, the differences were colossal. Decades later, fighter pilots still live by the axiom

SCRAMBLED – by Martin Richard

born in the thin air of World War I: *Speed is Life*. But just as the machines used to perform their violent profession have evolved, so too has the intent of this axiom.

Today, rather than speed, fighter pilots speak of energy. A modern-day dogfight is nothing more than a complex physics problem. "Speed," in today's language, is revealed through the concepts of potential and kinetic energy. He who manages his energy the best and most efficiently will win the fight. We use geometry and energy to gain the positional advantage in modern-day combat aviation. Our mission, in its most basic sense, is to apply aircraft handling techniques to get comfortable with recognizing and solving various geometrical problems. Among them are range between our jet and the adversary; closure; nose position differences; and then exploiting the maneuvering area or turning room available. In training, we practice maneuvering in relation to the bandit once we are familiar with these sight pictures so that we can deny the adversary employing his weapons against us, defeat the weapons if he has shot, or employ weapons ourselves. But, how does this apply to business? Let's slow things down and head back across the Atlantic to the office of Tom Ginnetti. In this simple example, hopefully you can see how *Speed is Life* can be applied to anything for which there is an objective. It is a clean, uncomplicated illustration of how these axioms can be applied universally.

Mr. Ginnetti sat contently behind his desk, smiling. As the Director of Human Resources at a large manufacturer in Florida, he had just completed his last performance feedback. He was finally caught up. He used this rare occasion to contemplate his activities for the upcoming weekend. Then, out of the blue, his boss filled his previously tranquil doorway. He said, "Thanks for volunteering to be in charge of this year's Christmas Party."

Tom sneered. Ever the optimist, he thought, "If I am in charge of this Christmas Party, I will make it the best Christmas Party the organization has ever seen."

He got his team together, delegated tasks, and asked for lessons learned from the last Christmas Party. Next, he came up with a plan. Energy was at a fever pitch as his team set out to complete their tasks and, fortunately, time was on their side. So what do you think happened a week later? How about two weeks later? What about a month later? What happened? Life happened!

Tom's inbox filled to its previously normal levels, his assistant "volunteered" for several more projects, the company rolled out new client initiatives, and the event planner's children got sick! Life happened. What was Tom to do? Cancel the Christmas Party? No, he knew the team was just "getting slow."

As the leader in a high-pressure situation, it is incumbent upon you to get the energy level back to the point necessary to get the job done. Tom put on his silk scarf, looked to the sky, and went to work motivating his team. He knew that the value of the *Speed Is Life* axiom is that it can be applied to any task, goal, or objective—no matter how large or small. Tom reflected on the things that motivated his team members to produce results. One member never missed his son's sports events, so Tom arranged to coordinate a day off for a job well-done. Another member's car had been in the shop for a week, so Tom arranged for an "on the spot" cash bonus to help. Tom did his homework, knew his team, motivated them, and got the momentum going again.

The result was an exceptional Christmas Party! Tom documented his "lessons learned" and filed them for next year's party—for which he was sure he would "volunteer!"

It is a somewhat simple example, but I use it because sometimes we believe the "simple" things in life are also "easy." I can assure you this is not the case most of the time. In fact, most of the time we go out of our way to make the simplest things difficult!

A leader under pressure must motivate. In order to motive, a leader must start by asking, "What motivates my team?" At the same time, a leader must maintain a close watch on the level of energy of the team. Vigilance must prevail or you will find out too late that the energy has dropped to insufficient levels to sustain performance and the task could be at risk of failure. What Tom found is that it is much easier to perform periodic maintenance on the level of energy than to have to revive it with the power of an electric jolt from a defibrillator. As fighter pilots, when we see the energy level waning in our normal, everyday tasks, we say to each other, "You're getting slow."

These words resonate because they hold a much deeper meaning than when taken alone at face value. Harking back to the men who wrote the book on fighter aviation years ago, these words speak to the relative energy level needed to succeed. In World War I, it came down to life and death. Tom's company Christmas Party fell short of such ominous consequences; still, the lesson we can learn is that one of the leader's most important tasks is to maintain the momentum from start to finish in a given task. The lesson I have learned growing up in a high-performance culture, and imparted to my clients like Tom's company, is that if you can keep the energy level high, the chances of success are improved exponentially. It comes down to leadership; it takes effort, and demands your constant attention. Don't get slow!

Tom used the *Speed Is Life* axiom to motivate his team and maintain the energy level need to complete the task. He also used it to ensure that the job was done right, and the team had a good time doing it! Sometimes this axiom works in reverse. Sometimes the situation demands that you take control and slow things down. While the effect is completely different, the important part is that the component of speed is the driving force. In particular, when safety is involved, *Speed Is Life* may demand that you STOP and assess so the situation does not spiral out of control. Just as the newborn World War I fighter plane had a limit to the speed it could attain to ensure that the relatively frail airframe did not succumb to the stresses of in-flight forces, there is a limit to the *Speed* a team can reach in certain situations. This is exactly the situation I faced when I worked with the Raytheon Integrated Defense Systems Group in Tewksbury, Massachusetts.

The managers at Raytheon IDS needed a new approach to the issue of safety on the "floor." Their job is to make some of the most important components in the vital weapons used by those fighting the War on Terror. In my jet, the F-15, they make the radar and two of the weapons we employ, among other things. These are extremely complex, cutting-edge, high-tech parts of an incredible machine. I can tell you, as a consumer of the product they produce, I am happy that the workers at Raytheon IDS are on our side! Their work is beyond compare.

Like any manufacturing-related company, it is imperative that safety be one of their top priorities. Without a safe working environment, employees, product, and the company's bottom line suffer. As I spoke with their employee group, I related the concept of *Speed Is Life*, but tailored my normal message for their specific situation. On the floor at Raytheon, where the discussion is framed in terms of safety, *Speed Is Life* meant something different. Sure, there were tangible and important reasons to "go fast." But sometimes, it paid to slow things down, too.

By necessity, safety was a hallmark of their high-performance culture. Not only did the team have to focus on what they were doing, it was just as important to focus on the order in which they were doing it. Safety was an important priority on the floor, but it wasn't the only priority.

The first step, as in anything, was preparation. I asked the team members if they understood the expectation relating to safety procedures. Most of the time, team members "know" what is written, but sometimes there are team members who do not understand the expectation. To combat this, Raytheon had periodic safety checkups to clarify. They made it a priority to communicate the expectation. This empowered the team on the floor to think strategically and tactically about safety. I explained to them that if there was a dangerous situation developing, for instance, if a team member was deviating from standard operation procedures for no good reason, slowing things down provides a great way to avert danger. If the incident had already occurred, then slow it down by communicating and get some help, or mutual support if need be, to avoid making the situation worse. Team members were provided training to deal effectively with the most common types of industrial injuries and were empowered to help. In the most tangible terms I had ever been presented with, on the floor at Raytheon, and regarding the subject of safety, the axiom *Speed Is Life* was employed to mean putting the speed brakes out and slowing the situation down so that the safety issue could be resolved without hurting someone or making the situation worse. The idea was to mitigate the stress created by the situation, or to put a speed limit on it, just as the World War I plane had a speed limit. As you can imagine, there were a lot of moving parts on the floor at Raytheon, each conspiring to derail the objective of the day and hurt the team and the bottom line. Safety was an extremely high priority at Raytheon; without it there would be no chance to complete the objective.

By slowing down the pace when safety becomes the primary focus, the overall mission benefits significantly. Taking into consideration all of the elements making up a safe operation is staggering. Still, it is essential that the team at Raytheon understood the working environment and the threat to be able to employ safely. The team at Raytheon understood that in safety, *Speed Is Life* means that sometimes they must slow things down in deference to the stress associated with the harsh environment of the manufacturing floor. In compiling the factors relating to safety, acknowledging the threat level, and thinking both tactically and strategically about operations on the floor, they were beginning to recognize the critical importance of the second axiom of a fighter pilot, *Lose Sight, Lose Fight.*

Lose Sight, Lose Fight. In a dog fight, you must maneuver your aircraft in relation to the adversary's aircraft. In order to be able to maneuver in relation to the adversary, you must be able to see the adversary: you must keep him in sight.

When we fly into combat, our head swiftly darts left, right, up, and down constantly. We scan the airspace to find any threats in the air or on the ground. Once found, we can execute the appropriate maneuver to gain a positional advantage or defend ourselves and our jet. Being able to maintain visual contact with the adversary does not necessarily mean that we will prevail. But one thing is guaranteed: if we completely lose sight of the enemy for an extended period of time, we are certain to lose the fight. The key phase here is "extended period of time." To understand this concept, let's get back into our wood-and-canvas-covered flying machine of World War I.

As I mentioned previously, the primary mission of those flying over the trenches in World War I was reconnaissance. Pilots spent most of their time looking down at the ground and taking photographs. Sure, they had their hands full flying these wobbly, laborious machines, but their mission was clear and focused—monitor and report troop positions and movements. When you have one thing to do, it is easy to focus. As the mission evolved, however, mission tasks increased and the pressure increased as well.

Troops on the ground took exception to these airborne assets giving away their positions, so they started to shoot. When pilots from the opposing side began to carry weapons aloft, they shot as well. The mission had not changed, but the environment most certainly had. If the World War I fighter pilot wanted to succeed and stay alive, he had to keep track of more and more things.

Imagine that you are flying above the scarred battlefields of World War I. The sound of your sputtering engine mutes the bedlam on the ground. You reach for your white silk scarf blowing in the wind, gather it, and wipe the oil which dots your goggles and obstructs your view. The smell of petroleum and gunpowder dances across your nose. Approaching a few miles ahead is your objective. Signs of troop movements reveal themselves as you draw nearer, so you pick up your camera and begin to click away. A glint from your high three o'clock catches your attention. You stow the camera and see a German fighter sliding aft, maneuvering into a lethal position from high to low so that he can employ his weapons and make you into just another story to tell at the bar. Not today. You aggressively turn your airplane and slice towards the Earth. You execute a "low yo-yo" to exploit exclusive turning room and tighten your turn circle to negate the attack. He overshoots. You reverse and breathe a sigh of relief because the fight is now neutral. You take a moment to scan the sky to make sure none of his friends are waiting behind you for their shot. Your airspeed decreases to just above stall speed as you jack your nose up and trade airspeed for altitude. You glance to your left to see the bandit. His energy state is the same as yours. Good; you have created options. Your plane shudders. You are dangerously close to stalling the wing. You push the nose over and trade altitude for airspeed. As you slice the nose by stomping on the right rudder, the plane moves right, reluctantly at first, as it touches the horizon, and then aggressively drops, pointing Earthward. Your airspeed increases and the ride smoothes in thanks. Just then, you hear the pops of ground fire. By trading in your altitude, you have put yourself into the ground fire weapon engagement zone. In negating one threat, you created another. It's not your day. It's time to get yourself out of the fight and go home. You point to the west and push it up. A gentle rain begins to fall. The cloud bottoms come down to meet you, forcing you lower. In the heat of battle, you have missed the changes in weather. You whisper, "Uncle." Your only alternatives are to chance the weather to find safe territory or turn back into battle.

You can see that if you neglect or lose sight of these environmental conditions for a short time, chances are that you can still complete the mission and return home. But, if you totally lose sight of what is going on around you, bad things happen.

In a modern-day dogfight, I will often lose sight of the adversary for a second or two. If I lose sight of the adversary briefly, I can still fight, but I will not be as effective or efficient as I would have been if I had maintained visual contact. Sometimes it is just physically impossible to stay "talley," which is a fighter pilot term for "seeing" the adversary. Most people don't know this, but when I fight in a dogfight, I spend most of the time contorting my neck and back in the most egregious manner to keep sight at all costs. I strain to twist around and violently swing left to right as I fly my jet to the extreme. My movements would put any Cirque de Soleil actor to shame! When the physical limitation of body rotation is met, sometimes the bandit escapes view. If I lose sight, I use my experience and knowledge of the enemy to make an intelligent prediction as to the point in space where the adversary is trying to go. Based upon that knowledge, I can predict the bandit's flight path and reacquire him. In my F-15 Eagle, the basic fighter maneuvering in a dog fight is violent. If a bandit ends up behind me, ready to employ weapons, my initial move is to execute a high g-force break turn. I reach loads up to nine times the force of gravity during these turns. If I have not prepared for this pressure, the process of losing consciousness can occur. First, all color dissipates; your world is made up of muted black-and-white hues. Second, tunnel vision pushes from the outside in and results in a "soda straw" effect on vision. Finally, complete darkness. In the fleeting moments before passing out, I can still hear and feel everything going on, but the loss of sight is my final chance to ease off the stick and get blood pumping back to my brain. I execute this aggressive maneuver to try to get inside the bandit's minimum range so that he cannot shoot at me, or to displace him from inside my turn circle, forcing him to reposition and buying myself some time. A smart bandit simply repositions and drives the fight if he can. If that happens, I have to try to radically change the fight from the defensive position. One way to do this is to execute a "ditch" maneuver.

In a ditch maneuver, I roll the jet inverted (or upside down) and, while keeping the bandit in sight, I point my nose to a place in space where he is flying. This reduces the range between us known as the rate of "closure." It's just like "cutting him off at the pass." This forces the bandit to change his fight. Then I pull with all my might, within the jet and my body's limits. I am trying to force the bandit to radically change his path of flight, and in so doing, cause him to make a mistake. With such violent maneuvers, changes in flight path, and physical limitations, it is easy to lose sight of the bandit during these few seconds. But just like I said before, that's okay. The key is in knowing where to look to reacquire the bandit quickly. In a ditch maneuver, an experienced F-15 pilot starts his scan between the jet's two vertical tails at the back of the jet and high. We call this "6 o'clock, high". If the bandit is not there, the scan radiates from that point. Once I find the bandit, I can plan my next move. If I can't see the bandit within a few seconds, my next move won't matter because the bandit can operate back to a position of advantage without my knowing and with impunity, resulting in my untimely demise. In combat fighter aviation, we have one or two bandits to keep track of. In business, the threats are never-ending.

Every person in business knows the vital importance of keeping in sight those things that affect one's business environment. The difference is that in business there are many more threats to your survival. If you build homes, for example, you have to keep sight of the competition, the weather, building codes, land acquisition, interest rates, sales, quality, and on and on. If you are in finance, you have to keep sight of your client, interest rates, new products, regulatory restraints, consumer sentiment, market conditions, valuation, and on and on. The business that does not acknowledge this reality is doomed to fail.

One frequent way that companies "lose sight" is that they fail to understand perceptions. It is often easy to believe what you think—a mistake that can be fatal. A 2004 Bain & Company survey illustrated this concept perfectly. Of the participants, 80% of chief executives thought they were doing an "excellent" job of serving their customers. Conversely, only 8% of the customers themselves agreed.[8] Talk about *losing sight!* The problem comes down to perception. Unless perception is understood, business languishes.

Sandy Cutler, CEO of The Eaton Corporation, and a client, has a great story about perception that he tells to his Multicultural Scholarship recipients. The Eaton Corporation was defying the manufacturing world by thriving. His large-scale heavy-industry products were the key components of hardware all over the world. The Eaton Corporation is a diversified power management company and in 2007 had sales of $13 billion. It is a global technology leader in electrical systems for power quality, distribution, and control; hydraulics components, systems, and services for industrial and mobile equipment; aerospace fuel, hydraulics, and pneumatic systems both for commercial and military use; and truck and automotive drive train and power train systems. Eaton has 82,000 employees and sells products to customers in more than 150 countries.[9]

Back in 2005, Mr. Cutler was confused. The annual report told a story of a prosperous company with a sound balance sheet and a great work force. Even so, Wall Street analysts were critical of the stock valuation. Sandy thought to himself, "Are we missing something?" He was asking his people have we *lost sight?*

---

[8] Morris, Betsy. "The New Rules." *Fortune Magazine*, August 2, 2006. Retrieved from http://www.money.conn.com/magazines/fortune/fortune_archive/2006/07/24/8381 625/index.htm. This article is a bit dated, but I believe still very relevant today.
[9] Retrieved from http://www.eaton.com

He assembled his brightest minds and sent them on a mission. His marching orders? To find out why the perception of Wall Street was not in line with the perception he had of the Eaton Corporation. His "tiger team" closed itself in a room. They poured over annual reports, sustainment plans, strategic vision, tactical initiatives, and every piece of data they could get their hands on. They looked at every angle of the business model and employed every tenant of Six Sigma. After hours and hours of excruciating, gut-wrenching toil, they arrived at the answer. Cutler called a meeting to go over what they had discovered.

"So team, what do you have for me?" Cutler said.

The team leader stood with confidence, smiled, and said, "Sir, Wall Street is wrong."

"And," Cutler said.

"Uh, Wall Street is wrong."

"All of that effort and time and that's what you have for me?" Cutler said, with a confused tone.

He sent them back to work. He knew they very well may have arrived at the answer; in fact, Cutler was sure that the Wall Street whizzes were wrong. But his team didn't take into the account the power of perception. In this case, the analysts' perception had a direct effect on the stock price. The team lost sight. They lost sight of the effect of the perception and provided Cutler with no response to Wall Street. Cutler wanted a plan to refine the perception to align it with the company's success. There was an answer there and it was much simpler than his team had imagined. After some consultation and deep, candid thought, on their second try the Tiger Team developed an aggressive action plan to shape perception to align with reality. This was a fairly easy thing to do, but Cutler knew that perception change was a marathon race rather than a sprint. Slow, steady and purposeful action plans were what Cutler needed and, in the end, it's what he got. The key is not to lose sight of all of the moving parts.

Push your team to make time to think strategically while maintaining a culture of high-performance execution on the tactical level. This enables a leader and his or her team to thrive in stressful situations. By keeping track of the variables that affect your business situation, both externally and internally, you are keeping *sight* so you don't *lose the fight!*

As the internal and external forces mount, pressure responds in kind. Wouldn't it be nice if in your corporate culture you could count on the mutual support of those around you? Wouldn't be nice to know you had many eyeballs watching, or keeping *sight so you don't lose the fight*, rather than just your own two eyes? Of course it would! To fill this need, let's talk about the third and most important axiom of a fighter pilot, *check six.*

Check Six. In the movie *Top Gun*, over and over again you see two F-14A Tomcats flying very close to each other, chasing a bad guy or being chased. The pilots maneuver their jets chasing "Viper" all over the sky within incredibly close proximity and traveling at over 500 miles per hour. They swirl like flies on lunch meat to gain position and shoot their nemesis. In one fateful scene, "Ice Man" exhorted "Maverick" to move out of the way so he could "take the shot!" It's Hollywood fiction. First of all, if a wingman of mine is screaming to get out of the way while he has his finger on the weapons release button – I GET OUT OF THE WAY! Second, fighter pilots never fly that close together in tactical situations. The reason is simple: survival. I bring this example to light because sometimes (most of the time), Hollywood does no favors to the subjects it tries to portray. In the case of *Top Gun*, the idea of mutual support meanders its way through a volleyball game, a love story, and a fictional engagement with a MiG-28. It's no wonder people get the wrong impression of what fighter pilots really do. So allow me to set the record straight, because the idea of mutual support is the most important concept a new fighter pilot learns.

When the F-15 was designed in the 1960s, engineers began by fabricating the radar system. Once complete, they constructed the rest of the airframe around the aircraft's most lethal weapon: its radar. The radar system in the nose can see out in front of us many miles (in keeping with the *Top Gun* thing, I could tell you the actual range, but I'd have to kill you!). The canopy is shaped like a "bubble," allowing the pilot to see in every direction, unimpeded. I can see directly above me, to the sides are no problem at all; I can even lean over the canopy rail and see almost directly below the jet. Still, every weapon system has an Achilles heel.

If you sit in the seat of an F-15 and you look to the rear, you see the aircraft's only weakness vividly. Your "six low" is obscured by the muscular frame of the jet. Flying in the F-15, I use clock positions for descriptive purposes. For instance, 12 o'clock would be directly in front of me, 3 and 9 o'clock to each side, and 6 o'clock would be right behind me. When I go out on a mission, I fly about a mile away from my wingman. I don't fly tucked up under my wingman like they did in *Top Gun*. Not only does this enhance my survivability by reducing visibility, it also enables me to check my wingman's 6 o'clock and for him to check mine. As I fly, we do the "Brady Bunch" scan. Remember the opening to the 1970s hit series The Brady Bunch? In the intro, the entire family was situated in a checkerboard on the television screen looking around. I imagine myself in the middle and employ a methodical process to look at every Brady brother and every Brady sister, as well as Mr. and Mrs. Brady. In this manner, I search for adversaries up, down, and all around. If someone flies up behind my wingman, up from "6 o'clock," and shoots him down, that is not his fault; it is my fault. I did not "*check his six.*" I did not clear the area behind and below my wingman, the area he cannot see. As you can tell, I literally put my life in my wingman's hands, just as he puts his in mine. As Duff and I recounted to corporation leaders at Ameriprise Financial, "In Combat Operations, our greatest fear was not death; it was not being shot down. It was making a mistake which would lead to our wingmen being shot down." We are certainly not unique in having this fear. This is a sentiment held by all good fighter pilots.

The pilots of the World War I era were the first to find out the value of mutual support. As tactics evolved, missions were scheduled in pairs so that each aircraft had a wingman. The wingman role, on the surface, appeared submissive, but in truth the role was vital. First, it provided another set of eyes scanning the sky for adversaries. Second, it was a force multiplier if one of the two in the formation was attacked. In this case, the wingman could maneuver to a position of advantage and not only support his flight lead, but also dispatch the bandit. It enhanced the offensive capability and also bolstered the defensive capacity. In modern day aviation, mutual support is the foundation of basic fighter pilot tactics.

Today, we spend time debriefing every aspect of a mission. One important part that always needs attention is our inter-flight communications. In order to employ effectively, we need to be able to communicate effectively. It is no different than a business situation. What I have learned is the method of communication differs, depending on the level of pressure. Sometimes you have the luxury of being descriptive and sometimes you have to be directive. If I am the flight lead of a "two ship", or a pair of F-15s, with 80 miles between my formation and the bandits, I have time to describe the picture I see, the tactic I am going to use, and what exactly what I'd like my wingman to do. If, however, I see a bandit rolling in on my wingman from 6 o'clock high, the pressure level has just shot through the sky, and it's time to get my wingman moving. In this case, my communication is directive. Here's the difference:

(Descriptive): Slam 1, 1 group, bull's-eye 360 for 25, 15,000. Slam 1 target the north group.

(Directive): SLAM 2 BREAK RIGHT, FLARES, BANDIT 6 O'CLOCK HIGH 1 MILE!!

You can see the difference. If your team has time and the pressure is not high, you may be able to be descriptive. An example would be briefing your team on the game plan for an upcoming meeting with an important client. If, on the other hand, the pressure level is high and there is a compressed or no timeline, you have to be directive. An example of this would be a dangerous safety situation developing on the manufacturing floor at Raytheon, in which case you may find yourself saying, "STOP! PUT THAT DOWN AND LET ME GET SOME HELP. DON'T MOVE!" In either case, you are *Checking Six!* You are providing mutual support for your co-worker. You are watching out for your teammate. It's a simple concept! The only difference is the method you use, and the method is dictated by the level of pressure involved.

In a high-performance culture, this principle does not just apply in the air. In the fighter pilot community, we check six all of the time. If we see that someone has had a few too many drinks at the bar, someone will say, "Let me have your keys." That's *checking six!* If someone in the squadron has a big project they are in charge of and they are getting distracted, we will intervene. That's *checking six.* It could turn out that we were completely wrong and the person in charge of the project had more information than we did, but as a member of the team, living by the axioms that have kept us alive, it is our responsibility to speak out. We strive not to be *Top Gun* mavericks; we all need some mutual support sometimes. How can you *check six* at work? How about at home?

In all of the leadership training and development forums I have led, the *check six* axiom is the one axiom that is easily internalized. In fact, the idea of checking six resonates with my corporate clients without exception. I believe this is because the people I work with understand that if you help the team win, you all win. It is a selfless approach to daily tasks and serves to benefit everyone, including the individual. It is T-E-A-M 101. Other clichés that apply include United we stand, divided we fall;

we are more than just the sum of our parts; and we are fa-mi-ly! While it is true that some organizations stress teamwork and others stress individuality, there are always times when we need a wingman in the business environment. One of my oldest clients took this to heart after a comical incident.

William Lyon Homes builds fine residences all over the United States. After discovering that one of their high-end model homes had a pesky electrical problem, they started searching for the cause. The opening deadline was bearing down. Electricians and superintendents scrutinized the electrical system and ran schematics. Pressure increased. Finally, they found the outlet at the heart of the problem. When they unscrewed it for replacement, the true culprit was revealed. An ill-fated mouse had been electrocuted trying to squeeze its body through the maze of wires in search of a morsel of food. Once the crisis had been averted, the on-site superintendent reported to the president of the division via email, "We have corrected the problem. A mouse was trying to crawl through the wires and was electrocuted. I guess no one was *checking his six!*"

We need someone looking out for us as we embark on our daily tasks. Sometimes we are overcome by the events that life throws at us professionally and personally. Sometimes we just make things too difficult. Sometimes we set ourselves up to get zapped, like the mouse in the house built by Lyon Homes. To be successful under pressure, no matter the circumstance, we need some mutual support—we need someone checking our six!

Speed is Life. Lose Sight, Lose Fight. Check Six. These three simple axioms offer an approach to cultivating a culture of success. They encourage individuals on your team to think beyond the limitations of their individual needs, personal agendas, and their job description. They are tools to help your team think strategically, while enabling them to execute tactically. Keeping these maxims in mind will inspire your people to confidently begin to lead at their appropriate level within the organization. Once this important concept saturates your group,

you as a leader will be extremely well-positioned to implement my innovative ACE Methodology, giving your team a process to lead and succeed under pressure. Plus, these axioms are easy to remember!

I was tested on September 11, 2001 at the foot of my jet in the chaos of a war-time situation when Sergeant Joe Kelleher, intelligence specialist, briefed me on the air picture in the beginning moments of the crisis. "Opus, there are eight jets airborne with bombs on board..."

I had to control the competing distractions and emotions just to be able to listen to the data he had. I had to sift through the unreasonable and discard the chaff. I had to subjugate the unimaginable and focus on my mission. There was so much going on that if I failed in any of these tasks, the moment most certainly would overwhelm me and paralyze my actions. How do you lead and succeed in a situation like this? The answer starts at the beginning—preparation.

I've had clients tell me you can't prepare for what you can't see coming. Well, if you believe that, my advice to you is to get out of business right now! You must prepare relentlessly for the environment you are currently operating within and you must use your experience, knowledge, intuition, feel, and finesse to anticipate and prepare for what is coming—for what you can't see. Just as important, but often disregarded, is the fact that to be effective in business, you also have to get your team, your peers, your supervisors, and your subordinates ready for what's around the corner. In fighter aviation, the concept is called "getting your wingman to the merge." The merge is where friendly forces and adversarial forces enter the same visual arena. It is when the high pressure hits the highest point in an engagement. Because so much of our work happens outside of visual range, the merge denotes a specific point in the fight where tactics, maneuvering, and mindset change. Some fighter pilots thrive on the excitement of the merge and others are paralyzed. The reaction depends on training and skill set. Most of our tactics are designed to keep us away from the merge because the F-15 is a large fighter jet and is easily seen, but in a training atmosphere, the merge is cool! Surviving to fight at the merge is a challenging endeavor. But just keeping yourself alive is not the only imperative. As a flight lead, you have a responsibility to get your wingman to the merge as well. When I was flying with NATO in the Tactical Leadership Program, getting my wingman to the merge proved to be amazingly difficult.

The Tactical Leadership Program is an exercise which takes place in Belgium and incorporates all of the countries of NATO and their tactical aviation forces. When I participated in 1998, the blue forces consisted of F-15s from the United States, F-16s from Belgium, F-104s from Italy, Tornados from Great Britain, and F-4s from Turkey. During the exercise, the blue forces would lead the strike force on a simulated mission into bad-guy territory. It presented a unique opportunity to work with multinational forces in a tactical environment and exposed many of the pitfalls in coordinating such an effort. Still, it was a hoot! On a given mission, we'd have upwards of 40 aircraft swirling above the countryside of Europe. The objective was to gain exposure to large-force employment tactics and work with our allies.

Because we had the most tactical experience and the most advanced aircraft, typically we led all of the missions and got all the kills; hence, all the glory. We felt like the big kids on the block! During the last week of the exercise, the Italian F-104 pilots approached me. They said, "Opus, you and your wingman, you get all of the kills. We want to get some kills this week. I have a plan. You lead us to the merge."

I smiled, knowing exactly how they felt. It seemed that the fighter pilot attitude transcended national boundaries. I said, "Absolutely!"

I began to plan the mission for that day with the objective being to get a kill for the F-104s. Their inferior turning ability, weak radar, and bad visibility would make this objective quite difficult to achieve. I devised my tactical plan so that the F-

15s would exploit the capability of our incredible radar. We would keep the F-104s about 15 miles in trail. As we pushed from our marshal point, we'd offset the adversaries at about 40 nautical miles. Then we'd identify the group with the least capability. Today, we'd pounce on the French F-1s who were providing adversary support. We'd stiff-arm the Mirage 2000 fighters and spin back to pick up the F-104s and lead them to the merge, updating them with the F-1s position, formation, and altitude. The goal was to "talk their eyes on to ," or point out the location of the F-1s and get them in the position to employ weapons. Once they called "Talley," or saw the adversaries, we'd peel off as a visual decoy and split to attack the Mirage 2000s as long as the F-104s were in an offensive position.

I arrived at my jet and the Italians were waiting for me! They were very excited about the mission, but I had my game face on. They said something in Italian and started explaining how we would celebrate that night after our victory. I told them to stop and I reviewed the plan quickly, and then jumped into my jet. After checking all of my aircraft systems, I checked in with the supervisor of flying and then checked in the formation. I could tell the Italian pilots were excited to get airborne. We taxied out and marshaled in the arming area. It always amazed me to see the mass of firepower on the taxiway. We passed hand signals down the row, trying to outdo one another and sending one another virtual "high fives."

Later, when we were flying, our anticipation grew as we approached the time to leave the marshal point. The adversaries were split into two groups, side by side, with about 25 miles between them. My wingman identified the northern-most group as the F-1s and we aggressively leaned to the north. At 40 miles, the die was cast. The F-104s were in position 15 miles behind us and things were proceeding as planned. At about 20 miles, I spun my formation back to pick up the F-104s after having made one last position call on the F-1s. As soon as we turned around, we could see the smoke from the F-104s engines. With about four miles between us, beak to beak, I called for my formation to turn "hot," and point at the F-1s. We offset from the F-104s so as not to give them away. We ended up about a mile and a half in front of the F-104s...perfect! My wingy said, "Two ship right 1 o'clock slightly high, 10 miles."

As my wingman and I continued to make positional calls on the radio, an exuberant Italian F-104 pilot called out, "Talley, talley, two ship."

I told them to "press," which was the call for them to proceed to the merge and the time we'd action south to attack the Mirage 2000s. The Mirages were bearing down on the fight and we had to turn towards them or risk becoming defensive to them as we prosecuted the attack on the F-1s. I called for my flight to, "snap 150," and my wingman made a hard turn to heading 150, which put the Mirage 2000s on our nose. Behind us, the triumphant Italian pilots called out, "Fox 2 kill the northern F-1!"

The other F-104 pilot followed with, "No joy southern."

He had lost sight of the other and his flight lead said, "Blow out heading 030."

Meanwhile, we were approaching the merge with the Mirage 2000s. We dispatched them in short order and I snapped my formation to the north to provide the F-104s with some mutual support. On my radar, I could see them blowing through the merge, about 20 miles off our nose. One F-1 was clearing the fight to go to the regeneration point. He was acknowledging he had been successfully targeted and would have to tag the regeneration point in order to play again. In training, we set up an arbitrary point to simulate the bad guys scrambling more assets in the heat of the battle. This maximizes training and teaches us to never assume we have the entire picture, so that we never let our guard down. The other F-1 was about eight miles behind them. Because the F-104s took an area equal to the entire country of Belgium to turn 180 degrees, the Italians decided to "blow through," or continue straight and escape danger. Their one kill would suffice for bragging rights for the next week, especially when the story was enhanced by a few glasses of Grappa! I advised them that the lone surviving adversary was at their 6 o'clock for eight miles and told them to "snap southeast" to help us close the gap between us. This would entice the F-1 to flow our direction and we'd clear the Italian's six. On our radar, we saw the F-104s turn and the F-1 followed suit. At about 15 miles to the F-1, we knew that the F-1 was the only show in town. I targeted my wingman on him and he quickly took care of business. As he called his kill, the F-104s screamed by us, rocking their wings in pride as if to say, "Thanks for getting us to the merge!"

Once we landed, the stories of conquest grew to almost mind-boggling levels!

Providing the environment for your peers, subordinates, and superiors to succeed is a vital part of being successful in a high-pressure situation. When things are getting dicey in your workplace, ask yourself if your tactical plan incorporates "getting your wingmen to the merge."

In applying my tactical methodology to leadership in high-pressure situations, businesses of all sizes can provide their teams with a practical approach to overcome the unique challenges that these situations present. The objective is to control the circumstance or situation, to capitalize on opportunities, and to execute successfully on a tactical level, enabling your team to succeed on a strategic level. These tactics were born and tested during while I flew over Iraq in Operation Northern and Southern Watch, over the rubble of the World Trade Centers on September 11th, and in the business trenches while negotiating big-dollar contracts. Living within a high-performance culture gave me the foundation for success, but in the final analysis, the responsibility to prepare and execute always rested firmly on my shoulders. Still, knowing that I was a part of a high-performance culture where people were watching out for me, supporting me, and giving me the tools I needed to develop and succeed makes an enormous difference. Is your team ready to execute under the most adverse, extreme periods of stress? Are all of your team members equally experienced, equipped, trained, and prepared? Who is *checking your six?*

If your goal is to be able to execute during a high-pressure situation, then you have to find out these things about your team. Building the foundation is an important first step. The next step is to equip your team with the tools they require to succeed. That is where my methodology comes in. The bottom line is that a high-pressure situation shakes out who the real leaders are. Because a high-pressure situation is consumed with emotion, it is critical that your team understands and executes my methodology. What I have seen in the business world is that in the absence of a methodology like mine, emotion causes teams to misperceive risk factors, value propositions, and action plans. Emotion also spreads like wildfire throughout the team, restricting them and causing inappropriate, impulsive, or misguided action. Finally, high-pressure situations trigger a domino effect on out-of-control emotions. The team's instinctive need to act will fill the void in a high-pressure situation, but unlike normal operations, inappropriate action can be devastating in a high-pressure situation. Pressure aggravates the effect of action and intensifies its implications. I cannot stress strongly enough that your team is going to act to counter the pressure presented by a specific situation, but without my concrete, rehearsed, practiced methodology, the situation can easily spiral out of control. Not only does my methodology equip teams permitting them to meet the challenge on their terms, it also walks through a process to capitalize on the situation and then learn from it. This process in and of itself allows for a constant learning system that will create the circumstances for a team to ultimately thrive in high pressure circumstances—whether they are dealing with your most important customer, or saving a life on the manufacturing floor.

Ultimately, the litmus test is in the results you produce. Even though I had never trained to shoot down two hijacked airliners acting in concert for the most coordinated attack on our country since Pearl Harbor, I was ready. I was ready and I wasn't even consciously aware I was ready, that is, until I arrived over Manhattan. *Speed was life* that day; we needed to stop the attacks right then.[10] We were presented with an unfamiliar set of circumstances and we knew that if we *lost sight* of any piece of the myriad environmental inputs, we'd be in jeopardy of *losing the fight*. Finally, we brought mutual support. Sometimes our wingmen just needed to be "there," in the correct position with the correct information. Sometimes our wingmen needed to intervene and speak up to prevent an egregious error, or to provide a calming, commanding voice to quell emotions. Either way, the lesson was that we had and needed wingmen, *checking our six* as we checked theirs.

I was prepared in part because of the three axioms I grew up with in my professional development. They are undeniably simple, universally applicable, and are based on action. It is a mindset and supports producing results under the most extreme conditions. Just as we have a foundation from which to live our personal lives, it helps to add to that foundation, expand it, and apply it to our professional lives. In the heat of the battle, I fought like I had trained. In the business battle, we have to go back to ground ourselves on the foundation we have cultivated throughout our professional careers. You may ask, "Why?" The answer is, you guessed it, simple. When stress, pressure, and expectation are introduced into the business environment, it becomes a new dynamic that tests you as a leader and challenges you as a person. What challenges you when you are under extreme pressure? How do these challenges affect the team dynamic? When I arrived over Manhattan on 9/11, I got a

---

[10] Although I have no definitive evidence, I believe there were probably other airliners on the ground which were not hijacked because they never had a chance to take off. My bro's, the FAA, and NORAD combined made sure that the attacks stopped.

vivid lesson on the unique challenges that a high-pressure situation brings to any event.

3

The Goal:
Having the Big Picture in Pressure Situations

"Wisdom is your perspective on life, your sense of balance, your understanding of how the various parts and principles apply and relate to each other."

—Stephen Covey

III. The Goal: Having the Big Picture in Pressure Situations

There was silence on the radio. I could feel my F-15 rumbling beneath me. My radios begged for attention, but they got none. I sat in my F-15 in disbelief as I saw Manhattan completely covered in dust, smoke, and debris. I assume the other pilots on scene were thinking the same thing, feeling the same emotions, and wondering what it was like at ground zero. Moments earlier, Duff, in the lead F-15, contemplated broadcasting to NORAD that anyone below the hit line of the second tower could be saved. The implications were that if he thought that from his vantage point, those with the restricted view from the ground probably thought the same thing and therefore more rescuers had probably run into the building. I saw the tips of buildings starting to reveal themselves as the cloud of destruction cleared. All of the sudden, I was back where I started the mission; I was praying. It was clear now that this had to stop.

I let myself be ill with emotion. I could feel it consume me. It threatened to make the situation twist out of control. I took a deep breath and tried to focus. For a moment, I imagined the building falling over on its side and thought that many, many people went with it. A call on the radio helped me focus, and slowly the level of noise began to fade back in and bring me back to New York.

"Panta 1, fast mover, low near JFK," New York Approach Control said in an excited tone.

"Panta 1." We made a left turn up towards Kennedy International, which was obscured by the smoke between it and us.

"Panta 1, we have an intermittent contact, low and slow just about 15 miles north of your position, southbound."

"Panta 1, copy. Panta 2, target contact over JFK, arm safe, flares hot, Panta 1 is split north."

I responded, "Panta 2 copy, arm safe, flares hot," and I pushed up the power to fly just northeast of JFK as Panta 1 rolled right and pulled away aggressively.

I could see a civil airliner with its gear down. To me, this signaled his intentions to land. I could not confirm this with the airliner, though, because amazingly, we did not have a radio capable of communicating with them. I wished I had. I banked over the aircraft and turned to the southwest to follow it in. I thought to myself that if the aircraft executed a missed approach, it literally was a mere seconds from Manhattan. It was a short and straight hop to the city. I passed in front of the aircraft, rocking my wings. I strained to turn my body and watched to make sure the jet landed while positioning myself between JFK and Manhattan. My thought process was that if the jet did not land, I could spin around to employ weapons. The only question I had was whether I would I have time to communicate the situation to NORAD and get approval back from them. My contingency plan was to try to divert the jet to the south, over the water, by dropping flares across the nose. In a worst-case scenario, I could shoot my 20mm gun across the nose to try to influence the rogue jet. Realistically, I knew either method would probably be ineffective. I called Approach Control.

"New York approach, Panta 2, we need to change the runway at JFK to keep the jets away from Manhattan as much as possible."

New York responded, "Working it."

I wanted to use runways 04 Left and Right because this would require the traffic to approach from the water, and in case a jet did not land, the pattern would take them northwest, buying precious moments. I figured in this high-pressure situation, having an extra few seconds might make the difference between life and death.

As I sped past the tower at JFK, on this pristine, blue, fall day, all again went silent and the world outside my canopy moved in slow motion. It was as if I were suspended in the air and I had lost the cocoon of my jet. I could see the airliner kick up smoke as its tires kissed the runway. That was a relief for the moment. Through the windows of the control tower, I could see that the World Trade Center was gone. I focused on the movement in the control tower. The people were above me. I could see them with their arms in the air as if to cheer me on. It was a moment I will always remember because for the first time that day, I felt as if I was starting to gain control of the situation. They needed us there, and they wanted us there. It made all the difference in the world. I rocked my wings with a new found confidence to tell them, "I've got it."

I was running low on fuel. I looked up and could see the KC-135 tanker high above me. I was roughly at 500 feet above the city that never sleeps, and the tanker was in an orbit at 20,000 feet. Air refueling tends to be a benign process, but it is never routine. Usually, a procedure of radio calls, deconfliction, and airspace release has to happen in order to conduct air refueling operations. Not today.

"Panta 2 is going to the tanker."

"Copy, Panta 2," NORAD and New York Approach acknowledged. NORAD understood that this took me out of their targeting plan for the next few minutes, but New York Approach didn't. Maybe they didn't understand, or maybe they didn't care. I suppose either was reasonable.

I crept up behind the tanker and opened my air refueling door. The boom of the KC-135 reached out to me with a lifeline of fuel. I eased into position, felt a gentle nudge as the boom entered the jet's receptacle, and I glanced that the fuel gauge. I was taking fuel.

"Panta 2, New York, there are three contacts in close formation over LaGuardia headed to ground zero, can you identify?"

"Panta 1, Panta 2, can you ID that contact," I asked.

"Panta 1, negative, I am on another contact."

"Copy. New York, I'll be there in one minute."

I hit the button on my stick to disconnect the boom from the tanker, slid aft, rolled inverted, closed my air refueling receptacle, and looked up to see LaGuardia. I pulled the nose of my F-15 down to about 45 degrees nose low and then rolled back upright. Just as I had practiced innumerable times before, as I approached the ground environment, I pulled the nose up so that the bow of my canopy was on the horizon, a maneuver called a "combat descent." I knew this was the sight picture for the jet's nose being 30 degrees nose low. As I headed northwest, I scanned the ground for the three contacts. Passing about 3,000 feet, I shallowed out my dive. At 2,000 feet I was 20 degrees nose low, and at 1,000 feet I was a mere 10 degrees nose low. This easy, programmed pullout allowed me to keep my energy state high as well as to safely transition to the low altitude environment. In the dive I switched my radar to "Auto-guns" mode. This was an auto-acquisition mode that would automatically lock targets within 20 nautical miles. As the radar scanned in front of me, I scanned around with my eyes. Just then the flashing "lock and shoot" lights lit up like a Christmas tree. I was locked to a target about 30 degrees left of my nose, co-altitude. I snapped my jet's nose to put the target 30 right for cutoff. I looked through the head's up display, or HUD, and peered through the target designator, a computer-generated box which surrounds the target's position. I could clearly see a three ship of Chinook helicopters in a diamond formation. Instinctively, I immediately threw the throttles to idle and changed my intercept to lag their position, or aimed behind their flight path, to control the excessive closure. I would have no problem running down a helicopter in my F-15. I approached on the right side of the three ship and rocked my wings to get their attention.

"New York, Panta 2, friendlies bull 010/15 southbound to ground zero."

A frantic voice came over the emergency frequency, "F-15 intercepting the Chinook near LaGuardia, we are friendlies headed to Manhattan, DON'T SHOOT!!"

I responded, "Panta 2 is the F-15 on your right side, cleared to press, head's up, numerous friendlies in the ground zero area, all altitudes."

New York acknowledged my call. A problem was developing. So many organizations wanted to "help" that there was an influx of helicopters and personnel to the area—all of whom had no flight plans and were making for ground zero. We spent the next few hours identifying these helicopters.

New York Approach came on the radio, "It appears we are having the same problems in Washington, D.C."

I felt despair. With a delicate touch, the controller was telling us that American Flight 77 had just crashed into the Pentagon. This raised the level of risk even higher. What other cities would soon "have the same problems?" I lost focus for a moment, trying to think about the next logical city on the target list of the terrorists, but then came back to New York. I could not do anything for anyone anywhere else. My mission was to clear the skies of New York and I needed to stay on it. The four of us flew over the city for several more hours that day, identifying everything that moved in the air from our perch.

Soon thereafter, NEADS called Duff and Nasty: "Panta 45 and 46, we are going to send you home. You are cleared back to Otis any altitude."

Duff authenticated the order and headed home.

The constant battle to remain focused on September 11, 2001 was the challenge. Another significant challenge was getting the information we needed when we needed it. These two challenges raised the level of stress to the boiling point. With so many competing inputs, compartmentalizing and synthesizing this information was key to my achieving my objective. It was also difficult to understand the ferocity of the information I received. High-pressure situations present unique leadership challenges.

I tell my clients that I don't get paid to "fly" the F-15, I get paid for the quality of my decisions. During high-pressure situations, your personal decision-making methodology can, and will, become convoluted because of many overpowering external factors. On September 11th, we were late. The first thing we had to do was to stop the attacks. Until we did that, nothing else mattered. In order to stop the attacks, I had to get airborne and start "building the picture." In other words, I had to segregate friendly aircraft from foe. This was an impossible task, so in its stead, I decided to clear the threatened airspace. This was an arduous, tedious process, but it bought me time. Clearing the airspace stopped the attacks. From there, I could exercise control over the situation.

We had never been in this situation before, so Duff decided that the best course of action was to apply past experience and turn it into something we knew. In his decision to set up a DCA Combat Air Patrol with a point defense, in one fell swoop he overlaid all of the procedures, plans, and courses of action we had practiced over and over again. It gave us a rehearsed frame of reference and more importantly, a tool to control the inconceivable situation. We had been manipulating the controls of our jets unconsciously for hours. We weren't getting paid for that. On September 11th, we were getting paid to stop the attacks and control the situation. We were getting paid to make the correct decisions.

Making the right decision is a challenge in a high-pressure situation. As a leader, this will fall on your shoulders at some point. What method do you use to ensure that the inputs to your decision matrix are reliable in the most stressful situations? Do you understand how filters in your processes contract and expand under the weight of pressure? Does your team perceive stress the same way?

First and foremost, stressful conditions are a perception based upon a worldview. A seasoned leader with a wealth of experience in dealing with pressure-packed situations has a much higher threshold for stress than someone who is not confronted with these situations on a regular basis. The differentiator comes down to experience, but the equalizer is training. The U.S. Air Force has studied this phenomenon extensively and has developed an intensive training system to fill the void.

Several times a year, the Air Force hosts large exercises where pilots from all services combine with multi-national forces to practice in real-world environments simulating large battles. Air Force studies show that if a fighter pilot can survive in his first ten hours of combat flying, his chances of surviving a war increase dramatically. Having flown many times in these exercises, I can tell you that they are as close to the real thing as you can imagine. The units tasked to simulate the "bad guys" not only are experts in real adversarial tactics and employment, they also, in some cases, have at their disposal actual equipment of the adversaries. Simulating combat situations so realistically is an investment in the people who are going to be asked to fight during a war and it pays off. During my seminars, I challenge my clients to apply the same methodology to their business development plans.

In one case, the simulations completed in my seminar allowed relationship managers in one well-known financial company train to stop high-pressure situations from spinning out of control and then to capitalize on the opportunities presented in these situations. I worked extensively with high-level supervisors to develop case studies for the relationship managers, based upon real-world situations. During the seminar, I set the stage with some background information, provided them with an objective, and then let them devise a course of action. We discussed the differing courses of action to see if they lined up with the company's vision and the situational objective. Many times, this is where we'd have to pause. Until the course of action lines up with the objective, progress cannot occur. Once we had established a suitable action plan, we practiced. Then we practiced some more. After we practiced, we took the time to debrief ourselves in excruciating detail. Debriefing is difficult, but in order to get better, we have to understand and acknowledge our weaknesses. One relationship manager took this training to heart in his particular challenge as a leader under pressure.

In preparation for a very important meeting with a new, very large client, Carl asked me to put him through the ringer! Carl was a rising star in the company. He garnered my most noteworthy compliment as a result of his participation in my seminars—he was a "strong swimmer!" Carl took the training and applied it to his book of business. He was not afraid to look inward, acknowledge the information that I presented, and figure out how he could use it to produce results.

I played the role of the client and we approached the task with his team the same way in which we had trained. His team started by defining the specific objective for the meeting and then devised a plan to meet this objective. Several times they had to go back to the drawing board to tweak the plan to ensure that it truly gave them a vehicle to achieve the objective. Once complete and rehearsed, it was time to debrief. In the debriefing, something very interesting came to light. It seemed that the relationship manager had a problem with the rote organization of the meeting. He would skip around the pseudo-script that his team had prepared, which led him to omitting key points of the plan. Without making these key points, there was no way the objective of the meeting could be met. This was a direct result of the pressure he felt. In the debrief, I suggested that he develop a briefing guide, or sort of super agenda, AND STICK TO IT! Obviously, in his role as a relationship manager, he had to be prepared to venture anywhere the client wanted to go, but if the meeting was to be a success, the briefing guide could provide a tool to keep on track. On the day of the meeting, I called the relationship manager to *check his six*. He and his team were ready and excited to meet with the new client. I knew his meeting was scheduled to last one hour and I asked him if he thought he'd complete his meeting on time.

"I will end on time, but I don't know where this client is going to take me, so I am not too sure we'll get to everything," he said unconfidently.

I reiterated how important it was to complete his objective and that he not only had a great team, a great plan, and a tool to stay on track, but I reminded him that he was ready for anything the client handed him. We reviewed the three axioms and then I told him to call me when he got a chance — after he debriefed with his team!

The next day I received a call from Carl. He was elated! His meeting had been a great success. He not only hit every point he had planned to hit, he had been so efficient that he ended up having 15 minutes at the end of the meeting for "relationship building." What else should a relationship manager with a new client be doing! In our debrief, he told me that he had anticipated the meeting to spill over at least 20 minutes. He had a contingency plan with his team in case things went poorly. He did not have a contingency plan if things went better than planned! A week later, the client contacted him and said his company wanted to move forward. Carl was amazed. His expectation was that he'd need at least six months and several more meetings to get the client to move. He was confident he'd get the client, but he certainly did not believe it would be this quickly. When I asked why he thought the client moved so swiftly, he said it was primarily because his company provided the best match of service and product for the client. But just as importantly, he said that the meeting had gone so well that his client expressed a sense of purpose, comfort, and reassurance that compelled him to move. Carl faced his challenge through preparation. Most importantly, he wasn't afraid to ask for help.

How much more money did the client bring to the table by moving six months sooner than anticipated? How much opportunity was seized by having time at the end of the meeting to "build the relationship"? These seem like simple, obvious tasks, but how many presentations have you sat through, rolling your eyes as the wheels came off the bus? How many meetings have stalled in a morass of data rather than providing meaningful information—*Speed is Life*. How many times have key parts of the meeting been omitted or glossed over because of time constraints—*Lose Sight, Lose Fight*. How many times has one presenter flailed in anonymity when all they needed was a little support—*Check Six!*

Some say that there is no substitute for experience, but in coaching some of the most talented people in business today, like Carl, my innovative training provides a suitable surrogate enabling individuals to use this methodology at their desk the next day.

I purposefully keep the definition of a high pressure situation vague and broad so that many diverse situations can be labeled "high pressure." On 9/11, we had practiced and familiar procedures and guidelines to specify a high-pressure situation and then a course of action to take. It was up to us to align those actions with the objective; that was the leadership challenge in this high-pressure situation. The country was counting us to execute. I want my clients to be proactive when it comes to pressure situations because it's much easier to slow down than to have to catch up to a high-pressure situation. *Speed Is Life*.

Have you ever felt like a situation was passing you by? Have you ever felt like you were missing things and details were slipping through your fingers? If so, you most likely were in a high-pressure situation. A high-pressure situation represents a challenge of the highest magnitude, no matter whether it is at work or at home, at your desk or on the softball field. The reason that it is so challenging is because people either act on impulse and emotion rather than on purpose, or they don't act at all. Whether you fall in the category of the former or the latter, the consequences are often drastic.

Acting on impulse in a high-pressure situation can make the situation worse. This is usually driven by lack of planning preparation and a lack of verifiable information. It leads to the typical case where teams start to act, but don't really understand the root cause of the problem being presented. Lack of action promises the same outcome. Sometimes teams are paralyzed by the situation because they are overwhelmed. They want to act; they may even understand the problem, but fear, pressure, and a lack of confidence result in inaction. These cases are typified by a lack of leadership and a "groupthink" mentality. High-pressure situations take a toll on the team's and individual's ability to solve problems because they are not comfortable in the environment. It is yet another component contained within the challenge of leadership in high-pressure situations.

When I am asked to consult with a team that is having trouble executing under pressure, I am always amazed at how different the personality of the team and its individual players becomes when pressure is introduced into the equation. For teams with no tool to handle pressure, or teams that have not prepared for pressure situations, in general a bad decision awaits. Bad decisions occur because through the lens of pressure, objectives, plans, and intentions are distorted. The result can be loss of revenue, loss of a client, injured team members, loss of job security, undue scrutiny...you get the picture. One thing is for sure: I have observed how pressure can snowball, its effect becoming more pronounced the closer a team gets to the deadline or action point. In flying, we call this "hanging on to the stab." Sometimes in the air during a mission, things are happening so quickly that the pilot feels like he is outside of the cockpit, holding on for dear life to the stabilator, the very last part of the jet, as it travels through the sky. This metaphor expresses feelings of loss of control, indecision, and ineffectiveness. In a leadership role, no one wants to "just be along for the ride." In its most extreme cases, I have seen high pressure affect individuals in remarkable ways, causing people to lose focus, trade morals for quick fixes, and even lose sight of their own personal values. Obviously, the consequences here are devastating. The good news is that with a slight change in the approach to pressure situations, the team and the individual can thrive! No longer will fear and trepidation dictate the situation, but with a minor alteration to the stress created by pressure, teams can execute in the most menacing environment. I am not saying that mistakes won't be made. We all make mistakes. The key difference is that, with my methodology, teams take determined action in support of their objective and thereby give themselves the chance to succeed without doing something dumb, dangerous, or significantly different. A perfect example of how stress challenges teams in the heat of battle happened to a friend of mine in an F-15E on a normal training mission.

The F-15E has become the workhorse of the Air Force. It is an amazing machine, capable of both fighting in the air-to-air arena and dropping precision-guided munitions on high-value targets. The F-15E has a crew of two—a pilot and a weapons systems officer (WSO)—who sit in tandem. Once a WSO friend of mine was heading back to his base from a training mission. The pilot reported that everything seemed normal as the field came in sight. Just then, the voice warning tone, "bitching Betty" as it is amusingly called, announced, "ENGINE FIRE LEFT, ENGINE FIRE LEFT." The pilot calmly reported the problem to air traffic control, notified the supervisor of flying, and prepared to run the checklist. My friend analyzed the situation and determined by the trail of smoke behind them that they were indeed on fire! He quickly opened the checklist and began to read. Step two of the checklist is to shut the engine off to cut off the ignition source to the fire. The F-15E flies fine on one engine, but the pressure was imperceptibly building. My friend kept his cranium buried in the checklist as the miles to the base clicked down. It was a clear day with light winds; this one was going to be a piece of cake. They called for a "chase" ship to rejoin with them and check the exterior of the jet. Their wingman reported smoke from the left side and the pilot of the crippled aircraft reached for the troubled throttle to shut the engine off. He pulled the engine to idle, then pulled up on the throttle to clear the detent and shut it off. As my friend monitored the left engine, he saw no change. Puzzled, he looked down at the throttles on the other side of the cockpit and saw the left engine at about 80% thrust and the right engine off. He gasped. The pilot, who had practiced this in the simulator many, many times, had shut down the wrong engine. Luckily, he quickly restarted the right engine and shut off the left, taking care of the fire. They landed without incident. Pressure had built to the point where a mistake was made. The reason it built was because my friend and his pilot did not acknowledge the situation—it was supposed to be a piece of cake! This is exactly when a high-pressure situation, disguised as a piece of cake, affects the outcome. *Lose Sight, Lose Fight.*

It is much better to have an individual execute my tactical methodology of perceiving the situation to be "high-stress," rather than to allow complacency and inaction lead to failure. Football provides another great example of this concept.

When a team is behind in a game, there comes a point when the clock is as much an adversary as an opponent. A good coach will sense this and transition his team to a "two-minute offense." Usually, this occurs with two minutes left before halftime or two minutes remaining in the game. Regardless, this is a departure from the normal game plan flow and acknowledges the external input of time as a point of pressure. The key is to acknowledge this early. While two minutes is a symbolic transition point, ostensibly to coincide with the two-minute warning when there is an extra "time-out" granted in the rules of the game, teams today transition much earlier to this hurry-up offense. Why? The answer is simple: time is a precious resource the coach is trying to preserve or use. Moreover, by changing the flow of the game, the coach is attempting to take control and drive the fight on his terms. He is acting on purpose.

His actions are based upon a rehearsed, familiar, scripted, and comfortable plan.

In combat aviation, our mission objective is always based on our risk level. The risk level is usually determined by planners above the tactical level because they have a bigger picture than the bro's flying the jets (usually!). It is an important tenet of how we execute a mission that the risk level is bifurcated from the tactical plan because in war, there are many missions proceeding simultaneously, most of which tangentially affect each other. Without the big picture, the actual risk level is impossible to gauge; therefore, it is determined for us most of the time. Risk level drives tactical employment. If the risk level is high, we may be willing to put forces in harm's way with the real chance of losing people and resources. If the risk level is low, we may opt for a real-time cancellation of the mission and come back to fight another day. The more thought we put into the implications of the risk level for the objectives, the more we mitigate the effects of pressure.

Knowing the challenges of being a leader in a high-pressure situation, it is better to transition early to my tactics than wait. Be proactive! In fact, successful football teams often transition to the two-minute offense whenever they need to change the complexion of the game, no matter how much time is remaining. While there is an increased risk in a hurry-up offense, sometimes teams need to try a different approach. In this case, the two-minute offense provides a known and rehearsed methodology to try a different approach and potentially get into a new rhythm.

In 2001, the New England Patriots, with their back-up quarterback Tom Brady, marched down the field in the final seconds of the Super Bowl. They were in their two-minute offense. Brady led the team closer and closer to the goal line, while analyst Don Madden chided Coach Bill Bilichek, saying "They should just sit on the ball and play for overtime." Bilicheck had a different approach.

The Patriot's two-minute offense had been practiced and refined. It was scripted, and Brady, who had never felt the pressure of a Super Bowl, thrived within the scope of the plan. The rhythm of the plan helped take the emotion and fear out of the decision-making process, and as the clock ticked off the last seconds, kicker Adam Vintieri scored the winning field goal. The Patriots confidently answered the pressure of the "big game" by sticking to their game plan. They executed the plan they had practiced over and over again, despite the counsel of Don Madden an iconic professional football coach. Just because a situation is packed with pressure does not mean it is time to get cautious, but without a plan that has been briefed, understood, practiced, and executed with confidence, you may find your only option is to "sit on the ball and play for overtime."

In the flying game of fighter aviation, we call this the "battle rhythm." The battle rhythm is a time line of the mission flow based upon the objective, the plan, and the internal and external inputs. In some ways, it is our two-minute offense. Because we practice missions in relation to this battle rhythm concept, we are comfortable not only with the plan, but also with the contingency plans for which we have prepared. In the heat of battle, there is no playing for overtime.

With this in mind, in business and in life, you must start by identifying the point at which a situation transitions from "normal" to "high-pressure." This is the key to the challenge of leadership under pressure. On September 11th, for me, the situation transitioned from normal to high-pressure when I was rolling down the runway, receiving my orders to shoot down a civilian airliner. I perceived this change in the relative level of stress because it was out of my comfort zone, I did not feel comfortable with the order, I hadn't ever visualized shooting down a civil airliner, and I had no access to the information I needed to synthesize all of the inputs external to my cockpit. I was holding on to the stab of my jet and events were passing me by. To be successful that day, I knew I needed to take a deep breath, slow things down, and understand that those who had given the order were checking my six. They did have the big picture, had followed established vetted procedures, and had consulted high levels of command to ensure that this was the correct thing to do. My job was on the tactical level. My job was to fly and fight like I had trained a thousand times before; there was no time to sit on the ball and play for overtime. What is your biggest leadership challenge in a high-pressure situation? In less obvious situations, how do you know when stress triggers a high-pressure situation? A good place to start is to define what a high-pressure situation is.

An F15 Eagle from the 102d Fighter Wing, Otis Air National Guard Base, Massachusetts over ground zero in the hours after 9/11.

4

The Question:
What is a High-Pressure Situation?

"When you start thinking of pressure, it's because you've started to think of failure."

—Tommy Lasorda

IV. The Question: What is a High-Pressure Situation?

Duff and Nasty were on the way back to Otis. It was the first palpable sign that we had regained air supremacy. The beginning of the end of that terrible day was upon us. I took a deep breath and went back to work. Bam Bam and I continued to clear the skies over New York and Eastern New Jersey to maintain control of the air picture. The next few hours were mostly boredom interspersed with moments of sheer terror. I circled over ground zero where smoke and ash was pouring into the skies. I surveyed the area around where the Towers had once been. Just to one side, I saw World Trade Center Building 7. There was fire coming out of some of the top floor windows. I didn't see much other damage in the area, but then again, I was going pretty fast. Hours earlier, my oxygen warning light had come on. My oxygen level was less than one liter, which was dangerous under normal circumstances. It didn't really matter today because all of our work was at low altitude where we did not require supplemental oxygen. Just then, I heard two of my squadron mates check in on the radio. "Huntress, Panta 5 and 6 checking in as fragged."[11]

Hearing Psycho Davis and Doo Dah Ray check in with Huntress signaled the end of my day. It was time to go home. I thought about how many hours my bro's had been on duty. They had been in the training mission I flew that morning. I figured the commanders had waived the "crew rest" requirements; we were, after all, at war. Psycho and Doo Dah would fly into the night perched in the calmness over New York. This ritual would continue for the next year as yet another paradigm shifted.

Defining a high pressure situation is a personal event. It is determined both by things you can control and those you can't. The role of a leader, therefore, is to be able to recognize the

---

[11] Translation: Our relief had arrived.

situation for what it is and then apply a methodology to accomplish the objective, given the change in the environment. You must bring your actions from unconscious to conscious, purposeful behavior.[12] Ask yourself: in business, how many situations occur on a daily basis that you would consider to be "high-pressure?" Do you react consistently to these situations? Why or why not?

When leading a formation of F-15s in combat, my approach was to stack the deck in my favor. I developed my plan to take advantage of my team's strengths and to drive the fight. Of course, the plan had to be in direct support of the objective, which would take into account the level of risk. My job as the leader was to give my team the greatest chance to emerge victorious and most of the decisions affecting the outcome, even in the supremely dynamic world of aerial combat, were made and practiced on the ground. The mission flow, position of forces, decisions to split forces, or mass firepower, depending on the threat, were all decisions that I made before I ever started the jet. Then it was up to me to execute in the air in real-time. *Speed is Life.* Knowing the plan inside and out is one of the keys to reducing the level of pressure. The unexpected events on September 11th combined with the risk in regard to the specific mission and objective before me, and so the level of stress was like I had never felt before. In the aftermath, I could tell that ordinary people could not imagine the pressure I was under that day. It was evident when the gates of the now-barricaded Otis Air National Guard Base were opened to reporters.

As the parade of media marched over my base in the days immediately following September 11, 2001, one question emerged repeatedly: "How could you shoot down a civilian airliner?" Reporters from all over the world wanted to know. The look in their eyes as they asked this question was telling. It

---

[12] "Act on Purpose," used courtesy of Sam Samsel of The Samsel Group, Braintree, MA

was a look of fear, uncertainty, and disbelief. It was a look that demanded an honest, composed answer with as much strength as it would have taken to carry out the orders given on September 11th. For obvious reasons, September 11th proved to be the worst day of my career, but as we fulfilled the endless stream of requests for interviews after the fact, it became painfully obvious that September 11th—"the day"—had become a definitive moment in the history of America. As a placeholder in history, it was an order of magnitude much the same as Pearl Harbor, John F. Kennedy's assassination, and the Space Shuttle Challenger disaster.

The fog of war and the reign of chaos had caused the wheels of bureaucracy to lag behind the event itself by a mere few minutes. If I had been SCRAMBLED just moments earlier, the end result might have been drastically different on a professional, personal, and historic level. I often wonder how my life would be different if I had been in a position to fulfill my orders; if I had been ordered to dispatch Flight 93 before the heroes on board had neutralized the situation. Even the prospect of that gives me chills to this day; the consequences— unimaginable. Still, on September 11, 2001, I wasn't asked to think it through. I wasn't asked to "decide" what to do. I wasn't asked to assess the situation. I was ordered to act. I had to apply the knowledge and expertise with purpose, unflinchingly, and flawlessly. *Lose Sight, Lose Fight.*

In my line of work, we practice our whole career for the one time we have to unequivocally, unambiguously, and without hesitation execute our orders, because when the order comes, we can't afford to get it wrong. We must remain focused because if we lose sight, we will lose the fight, which heightens the level of pressure we must deal with. As fighter pilots, we practice, we debrief, we learn over and over again so we are ready when it is time to deliver results. It is not hyperbole when I say that for twenty years, I walked to my jet expecting to have the "perfect mission." In twenty years it never happened. Still, I'd rather step out the door expecting perfection and settling for excellence. This is a notion that reverberated with a group of New York Life Insurance people who asked, "What does flying F-15s have to do with selling insurance?"

"We both make a promise, a promise that in the darkest hours of a combat situation or a personal tragedy, that we will be there, ready to execute the agreement we have with our clients at a moment's notice," was the answer. They got it.

So, when everyone wanted to know, "How could you...," I knew that the answer was deeply rooted in the high-performance culture I was nurtured within. My corporate culture demanded and expected excellence. It expected that through your own motivation, you'd show up on game day prepared and ready to execute. It was on your shoulders and your team mates showed the way—*Check Six!* Being in front of a camera talking about our feelings was outside of our skill set. It was stressful. We definitely required smart people checking our six when the reporters ambled on to the base.

Individually, the reporters I spoke with were very professional and quite nice. It was obvious that there was a certain tone of disbelief during the interview session, discussing the events of the 11th. Because many of the reporters I spoke with were from Boston and New York, I made the assumption they'd known someone who perished that day. Still, the relationship between the media and the military was not a natural one at the time and I admit having felt a bit of skepticism about their motives. In retrospect, it was unfounded—this time. The reporters preceded the parade of politicians on the base. Healthy skepticism applied to them, as well.

Before interviewing, we met with Lieutenant Colonel Maggie Quenneville, the base's public affairs officer. Maggie's easy southern style and demeanor were perfect for her role as the Public Affairs Officer. Her personality was the antithesis to the fired-up fighter pilots she advised and that was a good thing. Because media relations guidance changed daily, she ran down the latest mandates on what could and what could not be said.

Some of it was common sense. Issues dealing with response time, capability, and our names were off-limits. Other things were left to personal judgment. I was not intimidated by speaking with reporters about the mission that day. I imagined that they were playing the "good cop" role and so I kept my guard up to a large extent. I just felt more comfortable being a bit defensive during the interview, and with Maggie listening in, I was confident I wouldn't make a mistake. We were training for this mission in real-time, which meant that the threat level was definitely high. Said much more accurately, we were thrown into the execution phase with little time to prepare. Much the same way I compartmentalized my fear and emotion over the carnage in New York City, I tried to focus on the question being asked and subdue the emotions of the situation. It was impossible, but I tried. I knew my feelings were taking their toll because I always felt exhausted after an interview. I never divulged the fact I was also a United Airlines pilot because I didn't want to open that can of worms. It was bizarre being on "alert" at the base and watching reporter Miles O'Brien from CNN on television. Over the television, I looked out the window across the flight line ramp to see him actually doing the report inside our hangar. There were benefits to the arrangement, though.

One night, when he stood in front of aircraft tail number 77-111 inside our large maintenance hangar, and in front of an enormous American flag, he called my majestic F-15 an F-18. I promptly jumped into the alert truck, cut across the ramp (to the chagrin of the security forces team), and corrected him on the spot! He set the record straight after the commercial break.

A paradigm-shifting change in mindset had occurred. Coincidentally, I had completed annual Security Training at United Airlines a few weeks before. I had to watch a video about unruly passengers to update my currency. In the video, an inebriated passenger chose the wrong door at the front of the plane and bumbled into the cockpit rather than the lavatory. The impetuous first officer started to chide the passenger and yelled at him to "get out!" Meanwhile, the polished, composed, distinguished airline captain stabilized the situation. He invited the wayward passenger to sit down and look at all the pretty buttons and dials. He made small talk about the passenger's trip and how the service in the back had been. A narrator broke in to explain that it was far better to diffuse the situation using idle banter than to challenge the passenger and make the situation worse. At the time of my training, I found this all quite reasonable. Truth be told, I just wanted to fast-forward the video and sign the training log. But later on, as I heard the screams of First Officer LeRoy Homer on the tapes at Cleveland Center, shattering the airwaves and pleading for the intruders on Flight 93 to "get out," I knew everything had changed.

I am not sure I believe in coincidence. The power of those words changed how our nation conceived of safety, security, and freedom. As with any situation in my life, I tried to take time to examine how it affected me and what I could learn from the situation. I realized I had taken the privilege of security and freedom for granted to an uncomfortable extent. Maybe now it was right to be a little more defensive about it, a bit more skeptical and a little more grateful for having freedom at all. It would be wrong to be paranoid, but it was fine to examine the lessons I learned that day and apply them to every aspect of my life.

As I entered the business world, I found that the concrete techniques I summoned to prepare for extremely high-pressure combat situations were the same responses I had when confronted with high-pressure business situations. The common thread was my response, which was always rooted firmly in action. While the stakes were no longer life and death, the challenges nonetheless carried dire consequences if I did not succeed. I base my success on the fact that I recognized what triggered a high-pressure situation.

My clients hire me to teach them how to help their team smoothly and effectively operate under stressful situations. In their own customized way, they too are asking, "How could you...?" They want to understand the process I use to come to a decision in a high-pressure situation. I explain that it takes the right culture, with a high level of tolerance for preparation, a clear methodology in line with the goals and objectives of the company, and a willingness to learn from both the mistakes and wins of the past.

When I do speaking engagements, invariably I am asked about flying high-performance aircraft. Usually, people want to know "how it feels," or they are curious about how fast the jet can go, or what it is like to fly upside down. I always answer the same way, "It ROCKS!" But in a business context, I take the invitation to talk about flying as an opportunity to explain a concept I learned long ago. You see, as a fighter pilot, we don't get paid to fly the airplane; we get paid for the quality of our decisions. Just as in any vocation, there is a spectrum of talent and aptitude. Our profession's requisite skill set is usually misrepresented by the *Top Gun*-like term, "we're the best of the best." I can state with confidence that most of the fighter pilots I know are in an elite group for many reasons. The men and women I have flown with in my career are in the top 1% of the professional population. But at the same time, each fighter pilot brings a slightly different skill set and approach to the endeavor. Some fighter pilots are in the mold of Tom Cruise in the movie *Top Gun*; still others exude a quiet confidence and prefer to stay on the periphery. The profession demands this diversity in order to ensure that we are capable of maintaining high performance. The only constant demanded from our culture is that everyone must meet the "standard." If you can't meet the standard, you either get the training you need to meet it, or you find something else to do. It sounds harsh, but in the big picture, if a weak swimmer needs more support to get above the bar, then it's worth the investment as long as you have the resources, time, and need. If the weak swimmer can't meet the standard, then you aren't doing your team or that individual a favor by prolonging the inevitable.

My experience has taught me a valuable lesson that should resonate with you as a leader: there are pilots who fly fighters and there are fighter pilots. The pilots who fly fighters have endured the most rigorous training and have achieved an elite status in the best Air Force in the world. On the other hand, fighter pilots are those who have achieved the same status, but are the people you'd chose as your wingman when you go into combat. You probably have seen the same concept where you work. There are people who sell things and then there are salespeople. There are people who play professional baseball and then there are baseball players. There are people who manage projects and there are project managers. The difference comes down to approach, attitude, discipline, results, integrity, selflessness, commitment, and being proactive. It is a laundry list of leadership traits, but look around your workplace: the people who possess these traits are probably the ones you want to have on your team in a high-pressure situation. Let's look at an example of a pilot I knew who flew fighter aircraft.

Laser was a great stick. He could fly the F-15 as well as anyone in the squadron. He wasn't the best pilot, but he was definitely in the top tier. His academic briefings were always insightful and accurate. He managed one of the most important offices in the unit. His role, aside from being a combat aviator, was to ensure that all training and evaluation requirements for the entire group were up to standards. Typically, only the best instructor pilots were put in this role. Laser was at the peak of a great flying career and he was a great guy. Still, Laser had a problem with discipline.

As long as he was at our home base, the "home-drome," he was fine. The structure and mutual support was built in at the home base—we *checked six!* But Laser enjoyed going to air shows. He enjoyed seeing other jets performing for the crowds. He loved to talk about flying with the public and to trade stories about his flying exploits. He represented the unit and the Air Force well and he definitely had a positive impact on whatever he was involved in. That is, until he jumped into his jet and it was his turn to fly down "show center." It was in full view of a scintillated public that Laser lost his discipline. *Lose Sight, Lose Fight.* He often "bent" regulations to impress the crowd. He flew a little too low or made a pass a little too fast. He deviated from the approved list of maneuvers to wing it, or "John Wayne it" in fighter pilot-ese. After some spectacular mishaps in the Air Force, including the infamous B-52 crash at Fairchild Air Force Base in 1994, everything a pilot did at an air show had to be approved at the highest levels.

The Fairchild accident findings showed an egregious lack of discipline by the pilot in command and negligence by his leadership. It was well-known on the base that the pilot, Lieutenant Colonel Bud Holland, was a discipline problem. This was the fatal link in a long chain of inappropriate behavior. The investigation showed that on the day of the flight, Holland flew well below the established minimum altitude, banked in excess of the limit of 45 degrees for a B-52, exceeded pitch limit angles, and executed several unauthorized aerobatic maneuvers.[13] Holland was known to have broken these rules frequently. So prevalent was his lack of discipline that he even made it a habit to illegally park in front of the headquarters building rather than move his car to the proper location. Lieutenant Colonel Mark McGeehan, a squadron commander on the base, had seen enough. He issued an order to his squadron forbidding them from flying with Holland. This was an unprecedented move. Only McGeehan would fly with Holland, if so ordered by the Wing Commander. It was a brave decision that cost him his life, but selflessly saved the lives of his men. On June 24, 1994, in full view of their friends and family, Bud Holland crashed at Fairchild because of a lack of discipline, and he took three other officers with him. Just as culpable was the leadership that knew that

---

[13] Portions from: Thompson, Mark. "Way Way Off In The Wild Blue Yonder." *Time Magazine*, May 29, 1995. Retrieved at http://www.time.com/time.

Holland was intentionally breaking rules and refused to do anything about it. Only McGeehan, after being told to "shut up and color," took action. Today, the accident is the hallmark training for military pilots regarding the dire importance of not only compliance with safety regulations, but also the imperative of correcting unsuitable behavior before it is too late.

It is said that all Air Force regulations regarding flying operations are "written in blood." Someone died from not adhering to them, and fighter pilots regarded them as insurance, while pilots who merely flew fighters saw them as handcuffs for someone else. Laser's exploits began to catch up with him. At one air show, he flew so low across the runway that onlookers worried for his safety—and probably theirs. A phone call was placed and before Laser made it back home, the die was cast. Laser tried to talk around the issues, and while he was in compliance with the regulations, his actions showed a complete lack of discipline. It was a situation that could potentially spiral out of control and cost lives. Laser was grounded, or taken off flying status—the worst punishment levied on a fighter pilot. He traded all of his hard-earned qualifications for a moment of indiscretion in the spotlight. His response to the self-induced pressure did not meet standards. Laser was a pilot who flew fighters. Laser was not a fighter pilot.

While I have no doubt that if I ever had to push down track, or go to war with Laser, that he'd perform flawlessly, I wouldn't *choose* to have him on my wing. I would never choose a pilot who lacked discipline to go to war with. Heck, I wouldn't even choose someone with no discipline to be my designated driver! You get the point. On the other hand, another pilot in the unit whom I had the pleasure of flying with was in all manners and ways the consummate fighter pilot.

Heater was disciplined; he was selfless, proactive, and a model of integrity. Heater was everything a new fighter pilot wanted to be. His skills in the jet matched the best in the squadron and he quickly became an instructor and evaluator pilot—the highest ratings one could achieve. And while he could fly the F-15 with the best, pilots in the unit wanted to go to war with Heater on their wing because he was a fighter pilot. Heater was not flashy or loud. He approached his work with a great attitude, no matter the situation. He wasn't perfect and didn't pretend to be. He got frustrated, and he was human, but what set Heater apart from Laser was that Heater considered even the "inconvenient" parts of flying fast jets part of the price of admission. In his own understated, quiet way, Heater would often say, "If you can't do the small things with no one looking, you won't be able to do the big things." He understood the risk/reward equation. This down-home Midwestern man was a teacher and a leader by the example he set. No matter the situation, you could count on Heater. He was the kind of person I wanted to go to war with—if I had to. Heater didn't just fly fighters; Heater was a fighter pilot.

To be considered a "professional," you don't have the luxury of picking the traits required. You either have them or you don't. If you don't, you'd better find someone who does and learn from them. I don't intend to propose that it's easy to be a professional or, like I said before, that we don't all make mistakes. We do. The question is: how do we handle mistakes individually and organizationally and how do we define a high pressure situation? More importantly, why did mistakes occur? For now, look around your team members and ask yourself which ones are the professionals. What makes a professional? Who in your office manages projects and who is a project manager? Then ask why? This retrospective is not meant to exclude anyone, but it is rather to highlight the difference— something you can file away when your supervisor puts you in a high-pressure situation and asks you to pick the team you want to tackle the next challenge with. It's a chance to slow down and think strategically.

Smart businesspeople make this assessment all the time. It manifests itself in different verbiage, but it gets to the same common denominator. I have found that the somewhat pejorative question, "are you a manager or are you a leader," sums up the sentiment accurately. Mind you, the business world needs both managers and leaders, but for their own professional development, I teach my clients to be leaders at their level rather than managers. It is much more then semantics; it is a mindset or an approach to any challenge. You've heard it before and you know the sentiment.

When I ask the business leaders and innovators who hire me to define a high-pressure situation, it usually evokes a response such as, "I can't define it, but I certainly know when I am in one!" The answer signifies a lack of control. Both defining and sensing a high-pressure situation are equally important. The point is to recognize the situation and take action. Those who act by doing nothing are doomed to failure because either the situation will control them or someone else will fill the breach. A major consideration in high-pressure situations is the level of risk is involved. If the situation involves very little risk, the leader may not feel the same sense of urgency as when there is great risk. In a high-pressure situation, the sense of risk is palpable. There are also many other characteristics of a high-pressure situation that come to light in the heat of the moment. All of these are indicators to help you "know when you are in one!"

Use the following list as a starting point for your definition to determine if you are in a high-pressure situation:

• Risk Level	• Stress
• Perception of Time	• Alignment of Skill Set
• Expectations (perceived or real)	• Access to Information
	• Experience
• Mutual Support	• Attitude and Approach
• Ambiguity of the Problem	• Level of Responsibility and Accountability
• Anticipated Relative Outcome	• Fear of Failure
	• Training

The level of risk in a given situation is a great indicator of pressure. The higher the risk, the more pressure your team will perceive. Defining the risk level from the outset will help your team react appropriately and will help them prioritize stress so that it does not consume them. Understanding the risk level helps your team either speed the situation up or slow it down. I am sure your company has many business units working on their definition of risk. But for you, what is your definition of risk? When is a situation high, medium, or low risk? How do you react to meet the risk level with an appropriate amount of effort? Knowing, really comprehending, the level of risk helps shape our perceptions of the time and event horizons.

Our perception of time is different in a high-pressure situation. Sometimes it seems that things are spinning out of control and we are just along for the ride, while at other times, events unfold in slow motion. You feel SCRAMBLED! I have never had to eject from a fighter jet, but those whom I know who have can recount the process in extraordinary detail. To a person, they all say, "It was like everything was in extremely slow motion." Time changed. In fact, there is a psychological explanation for this phenomenon called "temporal distortion." It's real. Whether time is speeding up or slowing down, the point is that if your team perceives that time has "changed," then it is probably due to a high-pressure input. Keeping time "normal" with a fail-safe process will help mitigate this effect and allow your team to succeed. You can start controlling time by stating clear timelines and expectations.

Whenever a task is assigned, there are also expectations levied. These expectations can be perceived or real, and come in the form of goals, objectives, or defined performance targets. Sometimes, misinterpretation of expectation leads to confusion about the level of risk and can result in stress. This is the perceived expectation. By setting the standard in clear, unambiguous terms, your team can lessen the effect of perceived expectations and form tangible tactical objectives to achieve the goal. This is the real expectation and by stating it clearly, you are giving someone a powerful tool to succeed in a stressful environment. The higher or the more unclear the expectation, the more directly it affects the level of pressure.

Team members bring personal expectations to the table as well. We all have professional goals and dreams and sometimes a high-pressure situation is exacerbated or convoluted by the pressure we put on ourselves. This is a natural effect. It is important to be aware of and acknowledge this so it does not affect the process. Everyone has his or her own agendas; in fact, I like to call them "goals!" The key is that sometimes you have to subjugate your desires as an individual for the team. Notice I said sometimes, not all the time. I find that the clearer the problem to be solved is, the easier it is to rally around and plan smart objectives to achieve.

It never ceases to amaze me how many times teams start an action plan without fully understanding the problem with which they are faced. Remember the discussion of the helium Hula-hoop in my seminars? Usually, the result is self-critiquing! Defining the problem at the beginning and ensuring that everyone understands the problem will codify the strategy and planning to overcome the problem. It is critical to understanding where you are in the process and knowing when the objective is completed. Without a clear action plan, where each player understands his or her role, the chances of success are slim. This is a starting point and it forms the base to fight against uncertainty and ambiguity. Always start by asking, "What is the problem?" What question are you trying to answer, what challenge needs attention? Then ask someone else for their input!

We all would like someone to *check our six*. Sometimes we need more than one person. Having a built-in system of mutual support in your high-performance culture instills a level of comfort that helps the team succeed. Without some form of mutual support, the stress level increases. We may feel supremely confident and comfortable working alone, but working without a safety net can increase the chances that the results will be disastrous. It's that whole "I got your back" mentality.

The relative outcome of a situation also can be a stressor. If specific performance objectives are not identified at the outset, it will be difficult to know if the team has succeeded or not. In this case, people will perceive the outcome differently, which can lead to more pressure in the aggregate because it can lead to the team's taking separate VECTORs. Help by defining the relative outcome. What is the "end state" we are shooting for? When will we know we are mission complete? In my experience, unless everyone is on the same sheet of music in a high-pressure situation, bad things happen. These bad things are fueled by the power of stress. The question is, can you harness this fuel or will it just feed the flames?

Stress can be good or bad, but in either case, stress is a key indicator of the level of pressure in a given situation. Stress is internalized individually by the members of your team. Some people thrive on stress and some are weakened by it. Knowing how your team members react to stress and helping them to control the level of stress will help mitigate its effects. This is a delicate balance that you must pay close attention to, because typically, the people I work with will push themselves to the edge of the envelope. As they approach their limits, you are the safety net. They may not know where the line is between maximum performance and crashing and burning. Show them. Remind them of their strongest leadership-under-pressure attributes!

As your team members approach the limits of their skill set, or comfort zone, the level of pressure will increase. In my experience, this increase becomes exponential the closer you get to the edge of the envelope. As you push your team to perform, be cognizant of this. Be flexible and "fight your fight." Keep the goals and objectives in line with the team's skill set if possible, so that they can execute to their full potential. If you need to approach the edge of the envelope, do so with caution. The effects of a misstep can be multiplied and result in a disproportionate effect. Conversely, the situation may demand that your team members walk this line. The good news is that once they get the dance down and they feel comfortable, there will be a disproportionately positive effect that transcends more than the task that the team is working on. Keep the lines of communication open and provide sanity checks. Ensure that you provide actionable information to your team, not clouded by the misunderstanding of a high-pressure situation.

Depriving a team of access to information will increase the level of stress. The concept is called "working in a vacuum." Just as it is critical to identify the problem, it is also critical to seek out the information that the team requires. On September 11, this was by far our most formidable challenge. On the flight line at Otis, the information was so convoluted that I chose to disregard the details and focus on the larger picture. I was told there were "eight aircraft airborne with bombs on board," but it made no sense to me, so I parsed that message into something I could use as actionable information: we have lost air superiority, there are threats to Boston and New York, and I need to regain air superiority—that was my task. When your team does not have the information it needs, it cannot plan and execute. Barriers to communication in the team lead to stress.

As a leader, you must work to break down these barriers while maintaining respect for the chain of command. A simple way to do this is to acknowledge the administrative structure of the organization (the chain of command), while letting your team execute tactically outside of this administrative structure. In our high-performance culture, we use call signs as a means to this end. Using call signs works for us because it enables an air of informality within the formal rank structure. It works because it is a part of our culture. This will prevent the lowest ranking member of the team from "keeping a secret" because he or she is not empowered to speak out. When your team feels safe in volunteering information, take the next step and create training opportunities that compel them to participate.

If your team is dealing with a challenge for the first time, the level of stress will increase. It is imperative to seek out conditions and situations for team members to experience prior to being asked to execute in a high-pressure situation, if possible. Doing so will allow them to more comfortably execute and lessen the chance of their seeing something for the first time concurrent with you asking them to perform. This will enhance the chances of success while lowering the effect that this input has on the level of pressure. It helps you as a leader in high-pressure situations to cultivate a sense of "Been there, done that, got the T-shirt," and creates a feeling of confidence.

Attitude is everything. Every time I try to convince myself otherwise, whether in an F-15, as a father, or in business, I am quickly and usually abruptly reminded otherwise. The way a team approaches a problem can make all the difference in how it reacts to the level of stress. If a team is proactive, selfless, and has a bias for action, they will feel more in control of the situation. As a leader, cultivate this approach in everything your team is asked to do. This will pay enormous dividends in the heat of the battle. Let accountability set limits on your attitude. Let it be "that little voice" of intuition that either throws the team into full afterburner or rips the throttles to idle. Remember, *Speed Is Life!* Get to a place where you feel comfortable in accepting a task surrounded by stress with confidence!

The level of responsibility and accountability is another good indicator of a high-pressure situation. The relationship is proportional. The higher you go, the more stress has an effect because in the end, someone has to answer the mail. If that someone is you, chances are that you'll be under more stress. The more accountability you have, the more time you need to devote to monitoring progress and the process. The challenge is to resist micromanaging while maintaining control. I wish I had a

SCRAMBLED – by Martin Richard

dime for every time a supervisor I worked for failed in this challenge. If the situation is not going well, you may have to "shake the stick" and fly the jet to get your team back on track. If you think you might have to take control—I have news for you: you have to take control. It's like in the F-15 when we are low on fuel. We have external fuel tanks known as "bags" that extend mission time and range. They feed out first because they limit our ability to maneuver. When we are engaged by an enemy, we have the ability to jettison the extra weight and drag to meet the threat. We also can get rid of our bags if we need to decrease drag in a low fuel situation. Dropping the tanks gives us a significant decrease in drag. I always tell my new students that if fuel is an issue and you think you have to get rid of your bags, do it right now. The point I am making is that you began this thought process for a reason, and in these cases, it is better to act on purpose rather than to wait until you are past the tipping point. It doesn't do you any good to keep the "bags" if you don't make the airfield! The same is true with business. Realize that letting your team take the ball and run is different from turning them loose. They need a VECTOR. But, I am telling you, if you think you need to take control, take it. Let them throw the "micromanager" spears in the debrief. If you are accountable, you are accountable. Period. Don't let the fear of failure affect the fight.

The fear of failure can also increase the level of stress. Expressing an expectation of success can help your team internalize this attitude. If they don't believe they can succeed, they won't, and pressure will increase. Remember, have some swagger! You are on the team because you are valuable. Trust your preparation. As a leader, create a culture where your team is free from the fear of mistakes and can draw from the collective corporate knowledge base to succeed during high stress. If you don't feel prepared, ask for help.

If a team does not have the training and resources it needs, the level of stress will increase. Make sure your team prepares for any number of challenges by providing them with the training they require. Cultivate a culture of proactiveness by stressing to each team member that it is okay to ask for more training, more help and guidance. Acknowledge it, act on it, and the entire team will be better for it. Moreover, getting it out there will make the environment a much better place to work, too!

In today's accelerated business climate, most teams have adapted to dealing with high-pressure situations. They have done so by necessity and for survival's sake. Still others work at the edge of the envelope to get the jump on the competition. In practice, these responses are built to simply react to the situation if they are built at all. This is not good enough. Sure, it usually ensures that you can mitigate the consequences of a high-pressure situation, but it also ensures that most of the time you will finish firmly and comfortably in second place. This is not an option for my clients! I love that about them! I choose to work with teams who are comprised of bright, resilient, courageous, and optimistic people, who possess strong values, are fired-up big thinkers, and most of all, are decisive passionate team players. Who do you want to work with? Is that who you are working with right now?

Those organizations that can operate in a high-pressure environment with confidence (notice I did not say comfortably) are the organizations which will capitalize on the opportunities that the circumstances present—those opportunities around the corner, or at the next merge. It starts by knowing what triggers your high-pressure situations and having a plan to execute based on purposeful action. These are the organizations that will lead markets and industries and have the most successful teams. These are also the organizations with the most loyal team members, having the most fun, growing together professionally and personally, and experiencing the least amount of turnover. These are important factors because "churn," or turnover, and quality of life translate directly to the bottom line in terms of cost. For instance, in the military we are often presented with a challenge as some colleagues near retirement. This certainly is not the norm, but sometimes as a person approaches the time to move on, understandably their productivity drops. This is not really a problem if they only have a month or two until they leave, but sometimes conditions are such that they can have over six months to go after the decision has been made to retire. In one specific case, I remember a senior enlisted member of our unit who was a fine worker-bee, but did not really have the skill set to lead the enlisted force in the building. After deciding to retire, she had about seven months until she would transition to civilian life. That's when "retired on active duty" syndrome set in.

Retired on activate duty syndrome is not unique to the military. It is marked by a tendency to do absolutely nothing at work except to collect a pay check! The problem is that it can have serious implications for the team. In this specific case, a new, fired-up airman showed up at the base with a great attitude. My first error was putting him directly under a certain senior enlisted person. I thought the experience and job knowledge would be a good example for the new airman to observe and learn from. Unfortunately, this was not the case. The senior person did nothing. She spent her days delegating all of her tasks to the new airman who was not equipped to complete them. As a result, he became frustrated. Every time he had a question or was not sure what to do, his supervisor was nowhere to be found. Exacerbated, he came to my office requesting to be transferred. I realized my error. The challenge was evident and I felt the pressure. Move this airman with great potential or discipline the most senior enlisted person in the unit who was retiring soon anyway? My choice was clear and everybody was watching. The first thing I did was to deal with the airman. It had to be a decisive and significant action in order to keep him motivated to perform. Administratively, I moved him so that he'd have a strong, mid-level supervisor who was on his way up the chain of command. This move got everyone's attention. Having dealt with the immediate problem, it was time to control the situation. I counseled the senior enlisted person in question and explained to her that her actions were not only demotivating to the team, but also were having serious implications for the squadron's effectiveness. I was sure she did not want this to be her legacy as she completed a great military career. I reassigned her to several special projects I had and delegated tasking to her. Because her mind was understandably on other things, I made the guidance specific with very specific time lines and objectives. In return, I scaled back her overall duties out of respect for her position—as long as she performed! I felt in control of the situation, and the parties in question seemed to not only execute, but also to be happier. I debriefed the situation with my supervisor. The learning point was that I did not assess the internal environment correctly at the outset. I should have never put the new airman under the enlisted person with retired on active duty syndrome. I wrote the learning point in my continuity book and moved on.

Tactically, most teams are used to "putting out fires," but invariably they get caught up in perpetual firefighting rather than driving results by conquering the tactical problem. Most of my clients tell me that one of their biggest problems is that they have no time to think strategically because they are constantly dealing with the next crisis. By focusing on the tactical challenge, organizations can shape the challenge without distraction, plan for it, brief the plan, and execute the plan effectively. Then they can follow through by debriefing the engagement and learn from it so that they can apply the lesson to the organization's strategic goals. This leads to reaction rather than leadership. Teams need a tactical framework to shape the situation and capitalize on the opportunity it presents in order to effectively handle stressful situations.

When I arrived over the burning rubble of Manhattan on the morning of September 11, 2001, I knew that the terrorist attacks that shocked our nation had to end. Our risk level was the highest this country has known since December 7, 1941. We were willing to relax certain rules of engagement because it was imperative that no other airliners got near New York and Washington, D.C. There were many things to "keep sight of." First, I only had one heat-seeking missile and nine seconds of bullets. Second, our most precious commodity, fuel, was a huge problem. When we fly, depending on the weather, we have a specific destination field and an alternate field. The weather was fine, but we had to stay over the city for as long as possible. Consequently, we made the decision to use Atlantic City, New Jersey as our alternate. As the home of the New Jersey Air National Guard, they had the support we needed on the ground. If worse came to worse, I'd land at JFK, since it was right below me. The high stress caused by the attacks forced us to change the "rules of engagement," but it did not force us to deviate from any rules, regulations, or safety procedures. The more risk in the task at hand in a given situation, the higher the stress level. The same is true in business.

Another factor specific to a high-pressure situation concerns information. During stressful situations, information is essential. The dilemma in a pressure-filled situation is that information is impeded; it is incomplete, and it is sometimes unreliable. Leaders must anticipate and prepare for a lack of accurate information. Whether a leader trusts his or her instincts, or whether a leader has a contingency plan in place to deal with information, can be critical to success or can portend abject failure. My ACE Methodology provides a structure to consider the quality and flow of information during pressure situations. As a leader becomes more familiar with information challenges, he or she can plan for them and thereby enhance the likelihood for success. In my experience of consulting with the largest corporations in America, it is obvious that communication as a process, even under the most favorable conditions, is laborious. As stress is layered into the equation, communication becomes strained. Communication translates data into information. Under stress, this process tends to falter.

Communication becomes the first victim in a high-pressure situation.

Once you have identified that you are smack-dab in the middle of a high-pressure situation (or better yet, you have developed enough to see one coming), you'll find that high-pressure leadership demands agility and flexibility. There is an old saying in fighter aviation: "flexibility is the key to airpower." Simply put, when we embark on a combat mission, we relentlessly stick to our game plan with rigid flexibility...until it isn't working. Then, and only then, we will transition to a contingency plan to ensure success. Our past experiences and training give us the innate agility to change the plan on purpose rather than letting the circumstances control our actions. Flexibility is the means by which we mirror the quantity and tempo of change to react with an appropriate response.

On September 11, 2001, flying at one and one-third times the speed of sound, the risk level, coupled with the lack of information, combined to drive the level of pressure to critical intensity. But, when the controller got on the radio and said, "We're having the same problems in Washington, D.C.," the risk level became the highest I'd ever seen in my military career.

My first step was to abate the threat—nothing more. I had to neutralize the attack. I did not know who the threat was, where it was coming from, how many were involved, and what they intended to do. Still, the country was depending on me and the other pilots to stop this attack and I had to act.

I am sure at this point, you, too are asking, "How could you..." Here's the answer that became clear to me as I watched the second tower of the World Trade Center fall (sadly, the people on those airliners were already probably dead). I kills me inside to say this, and it's even more difficult to write, but their fates were sealed as soon as they stowed their carry-on luggage in the overhead bins or the under the seats in front of them. When those planes left the ground, there was absolutely nothing I could do to save the people on them. I could, however, stop the attacks and save those on the ground if there were other hijacked aircraft searching for a target. With this bleak realization, I could compartmentalize the task at hand and focus on the bigger mission. I get shivers even thinking about it years later. How could I? I had to; you were counting on me to. As for me being "able" to, that was a completely different question. Even though I hadn't practiced this type of mission before, I had been brought up in a culture in which I had been tested over and over again. The fighter pilot culture introduces stressors at every turn and demands the highest levels of performance. The relentless preparation in my professional development enabled me to subjugate my emotions so I could focus on the objective. I still had emotions, and I still felt afraid and unsure; I just didn't let that get in the way of me doing my job. I couldn't have that luxury in the air on the 11th; those things could be dealt with later at zero airspeed. At that time, I knew that my challenge was to make the right decision based on the information I had, given the trigger to a high-pressure situation. That was what demanded my immediate, prioritized, and purposeful attention.

The same principles that enabled me to deal with risk and lack of information when flying high-performance fighter aircraft apply to business—and to life, for that matter. The fundamental value of these novel principles and how they are applied is that they are universally applicable to any situation. Being successful under stress begins by being able to identify a high-pressure situation. Once a leader is familiar with working within the constraints of these dynamic situations, he or she can apply my ACE Methodology as a framework for success. My ACE Methodology provides a starting point and refined actions to deal with these situations effectively, and are based upon taking the appropriate action. The good news is that if you internalize these principles, anyone can lead and succeed under pressure!

My experience has proven that in combat and in business, preparation is critical. Be bold and passionate about your preparation—take preparation to an entirely new level. Script your responses as much as you can. Have a purposeful plan based on ACTION. Once you have a plan, practice it! "Chairfly," or visualize outcomes. Then, most importantly, debrief it. Learn from mistakes and successes. Think about what triggers your stress. What defines a high-pressure situation for you? Ask someone you trust what triggers a high-pressure situation for them and try not to get into scenarios; rather, investigate triggers as characteristics of the situation and list them. Once you have identified your triggers, as a leader, spend some time thinking about how your team deals with a high-pressure situation. How does that affect your leadership style and approach? I won't leave you hanging! *Check Six!*

5

The Individual:
How People React in a High-Pressure Situation

"Great and good are seldom the same man."
—Winston Churchill

V. The Individual: How People React in a High-Pressure Situation

When my jet broke ground and climbed away from the earth on September 11, 2001, I was awash with emotion. I unconsciously flew toward Boston, then New York, to chase down my assigned target, manipulating the controls of my jet through pure muscle memory. I was on autopilot—figuratively speaking, of course. My mind was overwhelmed by the complexity of the situation and the gravity of the world event. I did not have time or bandwidth to think about "how" to fly. Luckily, through years of preparation and practice, that had become second nature, much like walking is to most people. In fact, one of the most valuable tools that the Air Force had given me, along with my wings, was the ability to compartmentalize. Compartmentalizing is a tool which allows us to go at the appropriate speed—*Speed Is Life!* I was pissed off because I knew my country had been attacked and my colleagues had perished, but I also knew that now was not the time to dwell on that. I had to pack it away for later. If I wasn't able to, I knew it would consume me at the cost of the mission. It was up to me to compartmentalize in the bubble of my jet. I had to be able to control my emotions and actions, just as my wingman had to control his. It was a case where *"lose sight, lose fight"* was in play like never before. I had to stay focused, for me, my wingman, and the country.

When I arrived over Manhattan on the 11th, I could see the tops of the buildings poking reluctantly through the smoke and debris covering the borough. I was horrified. Having no frame of reference, I assumed tens of thousands of people had been killed. My heart raced and I got numb. I looked in disbelief and in vain for the twin towers I had seen so many times before. I tried to wish them back into reality, but it was useless. Then I started to get angry. I started to get really angry. I felt like I wanted to avenge this crime from my F-15. My mind raced. I became distracted. I could hear chatter on the radio, but I was not processing it. I looked around the city expecting to see other points of impact. I trusted nothing in the air. My guard was up and I could not concentrate. As my angst built to a crescendo, I heard a voice in my head calmly say, "focus." Time slowed. I took a deep breath and looked inside my cockpit at the engine instruments. My engines indicated normal—cabin pressure, oxygen, fuel, everything was normal. I looked at the artificial horizon that represented the earth in the middle of the instrument panel. It was one of the most important instruments in the jet. When we fly in clouds or at night and the horizon is not visible, we depend on it to display the altitude of the aircraft. It is a nondescript ball designed by an unimaginative, dreary engineer, with blue to represent the sky and black to represent the earth. But in this moment in time and space, it transformed right before my eyes. I could see the perfect blue ball of mother Earth in all its beauty and glory. It looked fragile, yet strong. It looked warm and welcoming and alive. It looked stunning and fertile. As the image began to fade, the radios became clearer. I heard Panta 45, Duff, coordinating refueling and altitude deconfliction.

I can't speak for the other fighter pilots that day and what was going through their minds, but I suspect the thoughts were similar. Still, on the radio, Duff was matter of fact and businesslike. I looked to my right and saw Bam Bam about a mile away, line abreast. His wings flashed to show the planform of the mighty F-15 and I snapped back to my cockpit. I knew I had to let the emotion go. I had to compartmentalize and I had to focus on the pressing issues.

The first thing was to calculate my fuel and loiter time.[14] Then I had to figure out what my role was in the current plan.

---

[14] Total fuel minus bingo fuel divided by fuel flow per engine per hour divided by 60 = minutes available in the CAP. This is the equation, but in a high-pressure situation, you have to keep it simple, so...the rule of thumb is: total

Everything else fell below my action threshold. Everything else could wait. Before, my mind wandered aimlessly with no VECTOR, but by prioritizing my responsibilities in support of the objective, now my task seemed achievable. It was time to get back to work.

In a high-pressure situation, the ability to compartmentalize is vital. It is the one tool that enables you to employ all of the axioms of a fighter pilot with attitude. It is a learned exercise. It is not easy. It takes practice, but I dare say each one of us has to compartmentalize to some extent every day. We all have to put "the bills" out of our heads during that important business presentation. We all have to put "what's for dinner" on the back burner in that important parent-teacher conference. We all have to tune out the radio in the car as we approach the next turn on a trip when we are in unfamiliar surroundings.

Compartmentalization allows individuals the ability to keep the big picture—or "photo grande," as we jokingly say. As the overwhelming amount of inputs bombard us in a high-pressure situation, they degrade our ability to synthesize all of the incoming data. The result is that our "photo grande" reduces to seeing the situation through a soda straw. Change the data to information and then prioritize. After these two steps, set the threshold separating your actionable tasks. Anything below the threshold—put it in a little container in your cranium and save it for later. Anything above the threshold—act on, in order of priority. In a high-pressure situation, your ability to compartmentalize can have a dramatic affect on the team's ability to work efficiently. Recognition is, as always, the key. How can you tell if you can compartmentalize or not? Most of the

---

fuel divided by fuel flow in minutes; even more simple: total fuel divided by an average of 100 pounds per minute burn rate. The point is, in the heat of the battle, a proven, tested shortcut that can save time, resources, and energy. What rules of thumb have you chairflown for a high pressure situation?

time, a true assessment of your skill set reveals the answer. But just to give you some mutual support, just to *Check Six* for you, here are some signs that you may need to work on the skill of compartmentalizing.

When I work with individuals during my Human Performance Consulting and Coaching engagements, I take some time to see to what extent my "wingman" or client can compartmentalize. The goal is to become aware of the individual's level of ability regarding this concept. It also gives insight into how I can help this person move to the next level of personal development—it helps reveal my game plan based on the individual's needs. I take out a one-dollar bill, a five-dollar bill, a ten-dollar bill and a twenty-dollar bill and arrange them on the table in front of my wingman, with the one closest to them in sequence, with about two inches between them. Then I say, "Your only objective is to fold the bills in half, flip them vertically, and then unfold them one at a time." Simple. I demonstrate and then let them do it. This is usually when they scoff at this exercise! Next, I tell them that the objective remains the same, but this time they must complete the task using only their nondominant hand. I tell them to begin and they usually smile and complete the task with a bit more difficulty. Now we're having fun! This time I tell them that the objective remains the same, but they have to close one eye and complete the task. A little more laughter, a bit more difficulty, but my wingman has no problem completing the task. I tell them that the objective remains the same, but this time there will be some external inputs at some point. I clandestinely pick up my stopwatch and slightly after they touch the first bill, I yell, "GO" and start the stopwatch. This usually causes them to pause and stare at me for a brief time and then hastily complete the task. I stop the timer and read the time and make a comment like, "that was highly average!" Quibbling from my wingman ensues. "I didn't know you were going to time me!"

I set up the exercise again and say that the objective remains the same. I fumble with my stopwatch for effect and reset it. My wingman perches over the bill like an eagle swooping over its prey. I yell, "GO," and start the watch, but this time, as my wingman completes half of the task, I start yelling, "STOP, STOP, STOP!" They stop. I show them the stopwatch clicking off the seconds with no action. Confusion follows. I start to call out the time louder and louder which usually results in action and my wingman completes the task with much more difficulty. Now it's time to debrief.

I go over the objective with my wingman and I ask if there were any questions before we started. I want to make sure the directions and objectives were clear at the start. Then we review the performance each time we completed the task and ask for input. Typically, my wingman says the physical restrictions (the hand, the eye) were annoying but did not affect the task much, but the introduction of the stop watch was distracting. Finally, the noisy commands had a substantial affect on his ability to complete the task. Now it's my turn to scoff! I ask my wingman to say the objective. I explain it did not matter how precise he was, how long he took, or how many "style" points he earned. There was just a simple objective, "Your only objective is to fold the bills in half, flip them vertically, and then unfold them one at a time."

This straightforward exercise helps me to demonstrate my wingman's ability to compartmentalize. If he truly focused on the objective, prioritized, set an action threshold, and executed, the distractions would have been put in a little container elsewhere. Sure, it is annoying having me timing and yelling and interrupting, but none of that had to do with his task at hand (just ask my two sons!). I challenge my wingman to do the task one more time, but this time I tell him that I am going to time him, I am going to make noise, and I am going to distract him. All of the rules remain the same and the objective has not changed. Then I wait. Usually, there is no action. I say, "What are you waiting for?" This usually compels them to begin. I start the stopwatch, jump out of my seat, and slam a book on the table. Sure it gets their attention, but for the most part it has no impact. Why? Because I told them what was coming (preparation), and I challenged them to put all of the distractions below the action threshold in a little compartment, to be dealt with after the task is complete.

So, take a moment and think about yourself completing your day-to-day tasks. When you are given a challenge, do those annoying external inputs that have nothing to do with the objective conspire to lure your attention away? Of course they do. It happens to everyone. We'd all be more efficient and effective if we could complete one task before moving on to the next. Now I know that life demands that we all become experts at multitasking. The difference is that during high-pressure situations, sometimes we will not be able to. Think about your ability to compartmentalize. Are you easily taken off task? Do you become distracted and quickly leave the task at hand for something less pressing? These may be signs that you need to work on compartmentalizing. Don't get me wrong: life constantly throws curves that require us to come off task to deal with another issue. BUT THAT IS THE POINT!!! If it is that important, it has taken a higher priority and necessitates action. Once that situation is dealt with, or when its priority has lessened, you can go back to the original task and complete it. Be aware of the conspiracy to get you off your game! In a high-pressure situation, focus on the objective, prioritize, and set your action threshold. Stick to it and you will be able to add this critical tool to your skill set.

It doesn't take a PhD to realize that people react differently under pressure. The more I am in high-pressure situations; the less I think we need a PhD for anything dealing with the execution phase! I am sure you can feel the sarcasm, but in all seriousness, I have found that in the tactical execution phase of a high-pressure situation, people can become drastically different from their normal behavior in day-to-day operations. Think about your own performance as you read these next few pages. Take a second and reflect on this: is your performance different when you are under pressure? Do you execute better or worse under pressure? We have a saying in fighter aviation when we step out of the training world and into combat. It is one key concept toward keeping alive: "Don't do anything dumb, dangerous, or different." Genius! Even in combat, we rely on the training, discipline, and rules to execute and come home alive. Two things to note here: 1) one way to stay in front of high-pressure situations as an individual is to keep it simple and make the plan look like something you've seen before; and 2) execute like you train. When I work with clients, irrespective of the industry, I see many reactions to pressure. I challenge you to think about the list below. Do you feel this way when confronted with a high-pressure situation on the job? Moreover, take yourself out of the work environment; do you feel these reactions when confronted with a high-pressure situation in life? This list is a small start ...what can you add?

Here are some negative reactions to high-pressure situations that require immediate action. I've worked with people who feel:

- ✓ Intimidated
- ✓ Overwhelmed
- ✓ Energy Spikes
- ✓ Fatigued
- ✓ Confused
- ✓ Angered
- ✓ Fearful
- ✓ Have Physiological Responses

When individuals find themselves in a high-pressure situation, they typically feel caught off guard or unprepared. Most of the time, I have found that this is a response based in emotion. Risk interpreted through the glass of emotion is a dangerous place to be. Emotion is definitely a component to use as an indicator. The challenge is to acknowledge it as a data point, but not necessarily as a point of action (as in "fight or flight"). The reason this is so important is because interpreting risk through emotion as a sole source, leads to the emotion becoming self-fulfilling. Danger! Danger! As you can see, the list above contains emotion-filled words. Acknowledge the effect of emotion and use it as a data point, not as a self-fulfilling accelerant.

As an individual, you can use these as indicators that you are entering a high-pressure environment. If you begin to feel these visceral reactions to a task, acknowledge them and then use them. Translate these reactions into data points to define reality. In other words, ask yourself, "WHY do I feel intimidated by this situation? WHY am I overwhelmed?" Seek out the answer and then go about the task of dealing with it. In coming up with a plan to cope with these reactions, you have a place to start in forming a plan to deal with the high-pressure situation.

The list of responses I compiled over the years above is in no way all-inclusive. I circle back to the Three Axioms with my clients to explain why these reactions manifest in high-pressure situations. By way of review, the Three Axioms are: *Speed Is Life; Lose Sight, Lose Fight; and Check Six.* When we consider the list of reactions, they usually are born from a perception of *Speed* (you'll often hear "things are falling through the cracks."). Sometimes they are a result of being uncertain about the objective (you'll often hear "let's get focused on the task at hand")—*Lose Sight, Lose Fight.* Finally, on a basic level, people feel isolated by the situation (you'll often hear "I am overtasked")—*Check Six!* So, why are these reactions common in high-pressure situations? Let's pull them apart.

Almost universally, when beginning my training, clients feel intimidated by a high-pressure situation. It stands to reason that if you can't control the pace of events, you tend to feel uncomfortable. Intimidation is the inverse of control. I tell my clients to breathe through their nose three times and hack, or start, the clock to combat this feeling. It does nothing to change the environment, but it helps individuals assert a small bit of control—albeit perfunctory and comical—over a situation. In taking action, individuals can push back that feeling of being intimidated. Inaction, on the other hand, will feed the emotions and further overpower you.

No other emotional reaction in a high-pressure situation is cited more by my clients than being overwhelmed. I am sure you have felt it. Being overwhelmed is natural when you do not anticipate events. The best way to deal with being overwhelmed is by prioritizing the tasks, using the objective as a guide, and to deal with those other items in order if possible. In business, this is not always a linear function, but to the extent you can VECTOR your efforts, close them, and move on, you will find you have diminished feelings of being overwhelmed. In any case, I tell my clients, "DO SOMETHING" rather than wait. Get an easy "win" to build momentum. Momentum takes energy, and feeling the energy of the situation is a common response to a high-pressure situation.

Have you ever been witness to a complete transformation in personality (good or bad) during a high-pressure situation? I observe this all the time and it is because the pressure of a situation and the emotions it elicits create energy. Energy can be used in a high-pressure situation for good, or energy can send you through the intersection ahead that has a blazing red light, right into a crash. In the flying world, thrust is good, but thrust with no VECTOR can be deadly. When you feel a spike in energy as an emotional response to a situation, make sure you use that energy in a productive, purposeful, and directed way. What is a productive way? It is a way that is based on purposeful action. There is always balance to the universe, and just as often as I see energy as an emotional response, I have seen its antithesis, fatigue.

Some people are drained by the fast-breaking events of a high-pressure situation. On September 11th, I remember that I felt this manifest as "hanging on to the stab." I was not flying the jet, it was flying me. In these cases, one is certainly not able to employ the jet as it is intended and the result is fatigue. It is the same in business. On days where everything goes your way at the office, you go home feeling much better than when they don't go your way. Think about the most exhaustive days you had: I submit that many of those were because an unanticipated high-pressure situation has taken all of your energy. Get up and walk around, stretch, yell, listen to music, jump up and down— do whatever it takes to smash those feelings of fatigue. You are going to have to be sharp to handle all of the inputs during a pressure-filled situation. Be on guard, because you have to fight fatigue or it will lead to confusion.

In a high-pressure situation, even when you have access to quality data, you seldom really know initially how to translate that data into information from which a course of action can flow. This, along with many other reasons, can result in confusion. Whatever the reason you feel confused, if you don't deal with it swiftly, it will lead to inaction. This is when you may have to acknowledge your weaknesses and ask for help. It may be that you just need to slow things down and get the "right" piece of the puzzle. No matter the case, confusion is a nonstarter because it will ripple through the decisions you make—and the more confusion, the bigger the ripples. Of course, there will always be some confusion in a high-pressure situation, but I have seen the most effective teams control the pace of confusion to stay ahead of its effects. *Lose Sight, Lose Fight!* As much as possible, we want to work on *our* timeline, not that which has been created by the high-pressure situation. If you let confusion reign, it will bifurcate the team, and anger can fill the void.

Anger is sneaky. Anger is an instigator. It rears its ugly cranium when no one is "driving the bus," when no one seems to be in control—when there is no VECTOR. What I have seen is that when an individual in a high-pressure situation grabs hold of anger for lack of direction or focus, it consumes them. I am sure you have worked with a person who is constantly assessing who gets the good deal and who gets the bad. Newsflash: these are the people who are always on the bad deal end of the spectrum...just ask them! Anger is an emotional response that fills a hole. It's like when I am messing around with a carpentry project at home and my wife says, "Calk is your friend!" I use the putty liberally to hide my "gaps." In business, anger and resentment fill the gaps if you let it. When I am leading individuals on a task and I sense anger as a response to a situation, I deal with it aggressively and with force. I review the objectives, delegate tasks, and most importantly, set the expectation. This usually pushes anger back into its hole. In extreme cases, you may have to separate individuals, but that comes at the price of efficiency. Deal with anger up-front, acknowledge it, and motivate the individual to move on. Finally, bring it up in the debrief and see how this response can be avoided next time. Anger is an active response to a high-pressure situation used by an individual to exert control. Fear, on the other hand, is its passive response cousin.

Fear is another emotional response that individuals feel when confronted with pressure and stress. The difficult aspect of fear, from a leader's perspective, is in a high-pressure situation I have found that individuals are great at hiding it. How many times has someone told you, "I was afraid," and you had not been aware of it? My theory is that people are great at hiding fear because they are so used to having it be a part of their lives—especially if they deal in high-pressure situations. I teach my wingman to acknowledge fear as a distraction. Fear exists for a reason; it keeps our senses sharp so that we don't die! If individuals approach fear with that mindset, they can use my tools to confront it and move beyond it. For instance, people are fearful when they feel like they are alone in a stressful situation. Use the *Check Six* axiom and show them that they have mutual support. It's the quaint cliché, "We're all in this together." Together, we will have a much better chance of compartmentalizing fear as a response. It is okay to be fearful; just don't let it get in the way of doing your job. While fear is the least talked about response, it is also the most difficult to conceal consistently. At some point, it will burst like the housing bubble. Fear exudes physiological responses like no other. This is a good thing for a leader.

Look at the individuals on your team. If you know them, figure out what physiological responses they have to stress. I have seen people who get pale, get sick, stutter, sweat, fidget, faint, shake, you name it. Sometimes they don't even realize they are showing physiological signs. As a fighter pilot, you really get in touch with the physiological responses of your body to stress. Because my F-15 is a single-seat fighter aircraft, I have to be cognizant of these responses because they are warning me that something is not right. Immediate action is required. Is my oxygen system malfunctioning? Is my g-suit working to help me ward off the forces of gravity so that I don't pass out? Am I just having a bad day because I am not well-rested? Whatever the reason, knowing my own physiological responses to stress are the indicators I use to act. In fact, the Air Force goes to great lengths to train pilots to understand their own personal physiological responses in the altitude chamber. The pressure is lowered internally to simulate the effects of losing cabin pressure at high altitude. Over a short period of time, your body will exhibit these unique responses. Taking note of your own unique responses allows you to recognize them when it really counts—at 30,000 feet! [15]   When I work with my business wingmen, I ask them to reflect on their physiological indicators.

---

[15] Because I know you are wondering, my unique physiological responses that I discovered in the altitude chamber were: 1) seeing "stars," 2) blue fingernails, and 3) feelings of euphoria. And yes, recognizing these responses saved my life twice in my flying career.

Knowing what they are provides great insight to the level of stress in their lives and on the job. Once an individual recognizes a physiological response, he can act. Use the *"Speed Is Life"* concept to slow the situation down, assess why the response is happening, and what to do about it—NOW! If not dealt with, anger, fear, and physiological responses will build to paralyze an individual.

Captain Obvious will tell you that the key to dealing with all of these responses is to keep them under some semblance of control, acknowledge them, and deal with them so they don't take you off task. The danger is that if you don't, it will jeopardize the objective. I have seen this happen many, many times. I can tell when individuals in a high-pressure situation are losing control because they respond to internal and external inputs with overreaction because their response is not proportional to the challenge—it is over the top. When I'm teaching a new pilot about flying in formation, I tell him the most effective way to be successful at 450 miles per hour, a mere 18 inches from another jet's wing, is to make small, smooth corrections. This is called the fingertip position. When a pilot gets good at flying fingertip, two jets move and react as one. It is a beautiful ballet of flight and the personification of mutual support. As an instructor pilot, you can tell when students get comfortable flying so close to another jet because they describe themselves as being "in the groove." Now add in some turbulent air, or a few clouds that the formation must penetrate—i.e., add some pressure. A typical result is that the formerly smooth student becomes stiff and ratchets the controls. Consequently, the student falls out of formation. In business, I say to individuals, don't let the pressure of a situation take you out of your groove. The first concept I carried from my F-15 to my business is that it is better to make a thousand small and smooth corrections than a few drastic ones. Big corrections add stress; massaging a situation adds a sense of control. Don't get me wrong: sometimes you have to manhandle the jet so that another one doesn't hit you! This is true in business, too. The situation may be so bad that you may have to step up and shake the stick of control, but if you see the high-pressure situation coming and can make small and smooth corrections, you have asserted control and built confidence, all to affect the outcome you purposefully have set out to accomplish.

As an individual, reflect on what your negative responses are to a high-pressure situation. Write them down, acknowledge them, and make an action plan to execute as soon as you see them manifest. Don't be afraid to advertise them to the people you trust. Ask them what they think your responses are in a high-pressure situation. You may be surprised! Let them check your six to help you move beyond their effects. I guarantee you that the few minutes spent doing this will pay immediate and lasting dividends. There will be a huge return on your investment of time because this simple exercise will enable you to deal with these responses effectively in real-time. Understanding your responses to stress will help you recognize them in the early stages and motivate you to deal with them before they derail your performance. It will also help you compartmentalize them so that their effects don't cause similar responses in your team. I have found that individuals have specific responses to stress that can be mirrored and amplified by the team as a whole if not planned for and dealt with.

A great story about President Harry Truman comes to mind in these situations. During the Korean War, he made the rules of engagement clear to his top general, Douglas Macarthur. To build perspective, you have to understand that Macarthur was as close to military royalty as we've had in the United States. His father was a general in the Army and received the Medal of Honor. He went to West Point, fought in three wars, and received the Medal of Honor. Macarthur's popularity in the public eye was unmatched during times of conflict. But, after publicly disagreeing with his Commander in Chief's policy on the Korean War, Truman was faced with a high-pressure decision. After reflecting upon it, Truman realized that

Macarthur's blatant disregard for the chain of command could not go unpunished, so Truman relieved Macarthur. This was a wildly unpopular decision. When asked by a reporter if he had lost any sleep agonizing over the decision, Truman responded, "Not a wink."

The reason that Truman had not lost a wink of sleep is because he knew himself. He relied on the values and morals that had served him so well in his life up until then. If you act on purpose based on the morals and values that make up who you really are, then you won't lose a wink of sleep either when confronted with a tough, high-pressure decision.

If you are having trouble with this, send me an email! I'll check your six! The way to really get comfortable with this is to prepare. Think about the task you have been given and what could interfere. Think about your own personal specific emotional responses and be aware when they manifest. Then repeat the objective over and over as you set out to complete the task. Take the negative emotional responses out of the equation but let the passion come through. Simple, right? Realize the importance of this because as you take your place on the "team," there will be more people, personalities, and inputs to distract you. You will add to the confusion. Pressure will feed off the environment. What you will come to find is that teams tend execute in relation to the collective reaction of the individuals. The danger is that in a high-pressure situation, time and space are bent! The rules of math don't apply. If individuals can't compartmentalize, the effect on the entire team is magnified so that 1+1 = 3 (cliché alert!) in a high-pressure situation.

You want to be the team member *Checking Six*, reminding them that if they *Lose Sight, they'll Lose the Fight*. Take some time to quantify your own, unique, personal responses to a high-pressure situation. Are they the same responses when you are in a group? Does a group take on its own unique personality of which it responds? Hmmmm...good question!

6

The Team:
How Groups React in High-Pressure Situations

"Some of us will do our jobs well and some will not, but we will be judged by only one thing— the result."

—Vince Lombardi

VI. The Team: How Groups React in High-Pressure Situations

Early in the afternoon of September 11, 2001, I was climbing through the still air to return to at Otis Air National Guard Base. Bam Bam called the controller, requesting to cruise back at 25,000 feet. The controller responded, "You can have any altitude you want; you're the only ones out here."

I looked around. He was right. I positioned my radar to maximum range. Nothing. Just then, the NEADS controller broke in and said, "Panta 1 and 2, we have a report of a light aircraft flying erratically 15 west of your position over Long Island."

Bam Bam acknowledged, "Panta 1," and we banked hard to the left and descended. I widened my formation positioning and set up my radar to look below me in the area that the suspect airplane had been announced. I descended to about 500 feet and, as my radar swept, I looked all over, but nothing was there. I called out, "Picture clear," and reported back to NEADS.

"Panta 2, copy, skip it, bogie 20 northeast of your position at 30,000 feet; do you have enough fuel to investigate?" NEADS asked.

"Affirmative," I responded.

Bam Bam and I reformed and pushed the power up. It didn't make any sense that a large aircraft would make it from the city, head northeast, and climb to 30,000 feet undetected. We both were skeptical.

"Huntress, are you sure that's not the tanker we just used over ground zero?" Bam Bam inquired.

"Unknown," they retorted.

We had switched our auxiliary radio to a discrete frequency so that we could speak to each other, but no one else could hear. "Opus, that's the tanker we just were refueling with. You've got to be shitting me. Do you have the fuel to ID?" Bam Bam asked.

"Affirm," I said.

I climbed above Bam Bam and had a visual with the tanker. I thought to myself, "How could they have screwed this up?" It was incredible to me that they didn't know this was the tanker we had just left! I closed into about three miles and could see the engines and the boom, which was good enough for me. Being low on fuel, I figured it would have to be good enough for NEADS as well.

"Huntress, Panta 2, it's the tanker."

Sheepishly, the NEADS controller responded, "Huntress."

On the way back to Otis, I looked down on the beautiful northeast. There was nothing in the sky above and an eerie calm on the ground below us. We began our descent for landing just southwest of Martha's Vineyard and could already make out the runways at Otis clearly. I positioned my F-15 in line with runway 32, lowered my gear and flaps, and readied for landing. The weather was still beautiful and the wind was light, but the blue sky looked somewhat muted now. What had been clarity in my life, like the sky, had given way to a film of haze.

There was a flurry of security activity around the base as the protection posture was raised to the highest level ever. Guard members streamed on to the base, most of whom were reporting out of patriotism rather than requirement. Two Security Forces vehicles, laden with weaponry, drove alongside me and escorted me back to the flight line parking area. I never have had that experience before. As I turned on to taxiway Charlie, I looked toward the parking ramp and the alert facility as I passed over runway 5. I could see maintenance personnel scurrying around the jets to get them ready for the imminent tasking. They performed standard safety checks, repaired systems if necessary, loaded external fuel tanks, loaded missiles and bullets, and serviced the aircraft. As a rule, this was a minimum of a two-hour process, and that was if everything went perfectly.

I did not know what our tasking was, but I sensed the next few months were going to be very busy. I was wrong. It was next year that was going to be busy. I didn't realize that the last training sortie I was to do for 2001 and for most of 2002 was complete on the morning of September 11th. From now on, we'd fly combat air patrol after combat air patrol over our own country.

I shut down my jet and slowly gathered my things in the cockpit. I was a bit stiff from the long mission and I gingerly stepped up on the ejection seat and crawled awkwardly down the ladder on the side of the jet. Earthbound again, I turned to my crew chief, who had a sullen look on his face. He looked at me and shook my hand. A simple, "Nice job, Opus," said it all.

"That sucked," I replied. "How are the jets?"

"They are all ready to go," Dennis, my crew chief said.

"What do you mean, all ready to go?" I asked.

"They are all ready, all of them," he replied.

"Amazing," was an understatement.

In the time that I had taken off and landed, the men and women of the 102nd had done something miraculous. They had taken 11 dormant jets, revived them, and in an unprecedented short time had loaded them for combat.

Under the most high-pressure situation that the 102nd Fighter Wing had ever been a part of, the pilots and maintainers had found a new level of execution. In their ability to focus on their own jobs, their own piece of the pie, they had outperformed any group I had ever been associated with. They were able to reach a new level of performance because they used the energy of the moment to drive focus on one objective—to make the jet combat-ready. They compartmentalized every other thing they had to do and focused on the mission at hand. And just as astonishing feats can take place under the most pressure-filled situations, so too can the most deplorable.

I touched on this anecdote before describing what I was thinking when I took to the air on September 11, 2001. Here, it bears a little more detail. In the opening days of Operation Desert Storm, most of the knowledge of how to fight a war had

---

retired with the Viet Nam generation. The new warriors approached combat with the deference that history deserved, but with a new vision of a technological battle. For the fighter pilots deployed to fight, the experience was being written with every passing minute.

Times were confusing. Most fighter pilots had spent their entire career training to fight the Soviet Union as the base line threat. Fate had different plans. Units were scattered throughout the Middle Eastern desert, now peppered with brown tents. In the Area of Responsibility, or AOR, squadrons readied for a battle that they knew was coming, but whose hour remained a mystery. Teams of pilots learned the local area procedures, studied Iraqi threat capabilities, and acclimated to the environment. Most were settling into the routine of being away from loved ones, the worst kind of lonely routine in which you were not privy to the date of your return. To combat the emotions, the distance, and the stress, fighter units readied battle plans and focused on the objective at hand—to win the war and come home alive.

In an F-15 unit somewhere in the desert, the commander called his warriors into the room and announced, "The war starts tonight. Is anyone afraid?"

Tim "Duff" Duffy and the other steely-eyed twenty-somethings and twenty-something wannabes in the crowd said nothing. "Well then, you are all a bunch of fucking idiots," the commander said with an unsettling calmness. Not exactly the pep talk that people who'd never been in combat imagined they'd hear!

He continued, "Scared is okay. Scared will keep you alive. Just don't let it get in the way of doing your job." With that, he left the unit to quiet reflection.

In another tent city somewhere in the Saudi dessert, an EF-111 squadron received the same news of the beginning of the war. The EF-111 is an electronic jamming jet. One of these positioned correctly could shut down the electricity and communications of an entire city. Its role in the war was to blind the enemy's air defense network so that our forces could enter battle undetected. But there was something else unique about the EF-111: it was an unarmed combat aircraft. Even so, it was a critical portion of every combat package. It was as critical as a good kicker on a professional football team and, just like the kicker, most of the time it didn't receive the recognition it deserved. It was so important to the combat plan that missions would be cancelled if there was no EF-111 support, but it was an oxymoron—an unarmed combat aircraft.

As a package of some 40 jets marshaled on the safe side of the line in Saudi Arabia, an EF-111 prepared its pre-push combat checks. All around, aircraft were refueling, the AWACS jet monitored the Iraqi air picture, and pilots all over the night sky prayed. The EF-111 crew of two nervously called out on the radio several times for position reports of the twelve F-15s leading the package. Their shrill tone on the radio confirmed their uneasiness. As "vul time," or the time the war kicked off, approached, their tone rose in pitch. Finally, the F-15 Air-to-Air package commander had no choice but to verbally chastise them on the radio: "We are as fragged; now shut up!" In other words, the F-15 formation was going according to the plan. Better to call out the EF-111 crew than to let their emotional response to the pressure grow like a cancer and permeate the package.

He was reassuring the defenseless EF-111 crew that the F-15s had the situation in control. The emotions of the EF-111 crew were beginning to potentially affect the mission's effectiveness and had to be dealt with harshly.

The enormous package of aircraft pushed in, completed their stressful missions, and pushed out. Targets lit up all over Iraq. It was an auspicious beginning to the war for the good guys. As the mission progressed, aircraft flowed south off target, some proceeded directly to their bases, and some refueled in the air. The plan was that the EF-111 crew would continue to jam the integrated air defenses to cover the flow out of the AOR accompanied only by four of the F-15s. As the border of Saudi

Arabia neared, the EF-111 crew was illuminated by an air-to-air radar. Their threat warning receiver wailed, and the pilot screamed on the radio they were reacting defensively to the threat. When F-15 pilots have a bro in "spiked defensive" mode, it is a big deal.

Two of the F-15s selected full afterburner and broke the mach to lend assistance. *Speed is Life.* They scanned the area with their APG-63 radar and could see the friendly, but saw no threat aircraft. The F-15s queried the AWACS, "Tiger 1, friendlies bull's-eye 160 for 75...otherwise picture clean, say threat to Jammer 1."

AWACS responded, "Picture clean." They saw nothing.

The frantic EF-111 pilot jerked his jet up and down and maneuvered aggressively against this invisible threat. It didn't make sense to the F-15 pilots. How could an Iraqi jet have made it to the Saudi border undetected at the end of the vul? There was no way. Still, the two-ship descended towards the EF-111 and continued their scan.

"Jammer 1, Tiger 1 is 20 north of your positions, picture clean, recommend flow south."

"Jammer 1 engaged defensive, unable."

The threat warning receiver in the EF-111 was vintage 1970, but since it was a first-generation technology, it could just as well have been decades older. It gave a general sense of who was locked on to you and threatening your jet, but you certainly would never bet your life on its precision. In this case, some spurious electron from a tower on the ground, or a satellite, or a side lobe from a friendly aircraft, was confusing it. Pilots in the EF-111 were trained to overlay a healthy dose of common sense to filter the chaff from their radar warning receiver. But that was in the controllable, evenly-paced environment of a peacetime training mission. In the heat of the battle, high-pressure situations give birth to the fog and friction of war. There was no threat. There was no danger. Common sense said it was extremely unlikely that the F-15s and the AWACS missed an Iraqi fighter that far south. Just as in the case of the confusion about our own tanker on my way back to Otis on 9/11, its position made no sense.

"Tiger 1, picture clear, Jammer posit?" The radio was silent.

"Tiger 1, picture clear, Jammer posit?"

In their aggressive threat reactions, the EF-111 crew had impacted the ground. *Lose Sight, Lose Fight.* They had used all of their airspeed in defeating an invisible threat that was not there and lost their situational awareness (SA). Pressure had its first kill of the war.

While certainly not culpable, it was obvious from the tone of the voices on the radio that the EF-111 commander had not given the same speech as the F-15 commander. He did not acknowledge that fear was not only an expected emotional response to this high-pressure situation, but that it was a natural response and, more importantly, once acknowledged, could be controlled or at least compartmentalized. It was a fatal error and the crew members let fear get in the way of doing their job.

The emotional response of a team to a high-pressure situation is different than that of an individual. In the case of the EF-111 crew, the risk they felt was based primarily on emotion. It was contagious inside their cockpit between the two crew members and could have potentially spread throughout the entire package. The domino effect was only broken with direct and aggressive action, but still had enough staying power to take two lives in end.

When I work with clients, sometimes the group dynamic is simply the sum of its individuals. In this case, dealing with emotional response becomes a simple process of identifying it, acknowledging it, and moving on. Most of the time, the team's response to pressure is less obvious. The reason is because team members do not act, work, and execute the same way individually as they do in a group. Sometimes, personalities are completely different in a group setting than they are individually. By extension, this leads to completely different responses to a high-pressure situation. Add to the environment the fact that individuals in the groups bring biases, perceive the environment differently, and feel pressure to incongruent levels and you have a mix of striking uncertainty!

As a leader in a high-pressure situation, you have put a team on a task because you need the mutual support of others to be a force multiplier. *Check Six.* You would think that a room of great minds would succeed when grouped together, but, as author Howard Bloom points out, the collective IQ of great minds actually decreases when assembled around a specific objective. Why is this? Bloom chalks it up to, among other things, the tendency of a group to adhere to implied social norms which can stifle innovation (not to mention limiting IQ). Somewhere in the "group" setting, individuals react below their full potential. They lose their individuality and capitulate to the social norms of the group dynamic. I am sure you have felt and seen this many times in your business careers. Here are some of the things I have observed while consulting with groups on performance issues. Sometimes people morph into being:

- ✓ Overly Assertive
- ✓ Submissive
- ✓ Opportunists
- ✓ Posers
- ✓ Secret Keepers
- ✓ Disrupters
- ✓ Low Talkers
- ✓ Sideliners
- ✓ Inertia Worshipers

In a group situation, sometimes otherwise calm, collected individuals become overly assertive. This is a manifestation of their passion for the task at hand in the best cases, but in the worst, can be an insight into fear or uneasiness.

Sometimes, individuals on the team become so passionate about their position that they feel the need to advocate for it in a manner that excludes input from others. This can usually be controlled by a leader slowing things down and managing the flow of communication. On the other hand, sometimes being overly assertive is a window into an individual's insecurity with working within a group situation. This could be because the individual feels untrained, unprepared, or unsure about his or her ability to complete the task. As a leader, you must communicate your openness to help, and your willingness to acknowledge that having these fears is okay. Help is available and there is no stigma attached to acknowledging that you need assistance. In a high-pressure situation, feeling unprepared is a common response. Sometimes an individual's behavior on a team in a high-pressure situation is 180 degrees out from their normal action.

Overly assertive people on a team have another considerable effect on the group: they overpower others on the team and cause them to become submissive. These team members respond to the aggressive behavior and the uncertainty of the situation by just laying low and saying nothing. They still can be productive members of the team, but their full effect will never come through. They eventually become too intimidated to speak out and their motivation will wane. If you see an individual like this on your team, you must step up for them! Control the situation and elicit their input by quieting the other team members and asking direct questions. When I am briefing a flying mission, at the end I will look every team member in the eye, individually, and then point to him or her and ask, "Do you have any questions?" I use this technique rather than just throwing out, "any questions?" because there is a much higher chance that a submissive team member will use this invitation to voice a concern or offer an idea. This gives individualized permission to overcome the tendency of capitulation to the group's social norm. Somewhere between being overly assertive and submissive lie the opportunists.

While being an opportunist can sometimes be a good thing, in this iteration, I am speaking of opportunists in negative terms. This kind of opportunist works to subjugate the progress of the group in order to appear to be the hero in the end. It can be debilitating for the rest of the team to see this type of behavior, especially when it's effective, because sometimes the team leader doesn't have enough situational awareness to see the truth. As a leader, I have found that opportunists stick out like a sore thumb. When I see an opportunist at work, my first action is to change the behavior. Opportunists can splinter a team into competing factions. An opportunist demands attention from the leader. You must manage the effects on the team by metering the opportunist's actions. Some techniques I have found effective are to assign the opportunist specific tasks and demand results. By keeping them in the weeds, you can monitor progress, let the opportunists make a positive impact on the task at hand, and segregate the subversive behavior. In a macro sense, when confronted with this behavior, I strive to make sure everyone understands that they have a stake in the outcome. If the team understands the expectation, the objective, and where they fit, they will see their stake in a positive outcome. This translates, in a broad sense, to mirroring the action of forming a team in the first place. If your team knows they have a stake in the outcome, they will do tremendous things for you. I remember that I was walking through the offices of a very large financial company in the Boston area in preparation for an extended consulting engagement when the VP, who was giving me the tour, stopped to introduce me to one of his star players. He talked about how much money she had saved the company and what a tremendous job she had done. In response, she said, "It wasn't me; it was my team." She got it.

Think about it: you know her team was listening. Can you imagine the effect if she had said, "oh, yeh, it was all me!" If nothing else, her team heard her distribute the positive feedback and that is just one part of their stake in the outcome—they have a leader who will *check their six*. In the worst cases, opportunists can undermine the team and overshadow their potential positive input. Posers, on the other hand, should not be on the team.

A poser is someone who exhibits behavior that indicates to a leader that they know what is going on when, in actuality, they don't. In fact—and here is the reason they can be destructive—they know they don't know and they don't care. They have a completely different agenda. This shows intent, no matter the outward reason for the "posing." Posers can take the momentum of the team off track and, in the worst cases, cause the team to assess information incorrectly as well as to misinterpret the real objective. Posers usually are vocal and are adept at gaining support on the team. All the more reason to be wary of a poser. They fain situational awareness, but it is built on a house of falsehoods. Their input can be unrecoverable, so they must be dealt with as soon as identified. As a leader, I tend to reassign a poser and get them off of the team, since this could just be a response to the pressure of the situation. You've seen it before: when the pressure hits, this person has to have all of the answers. If you can't segregate them from the team, a poser will need constant monitoring. Focus the team back on the objectives, and help the team see the landscape as it really is. Soon, the team will be able to police itself. As they gain control of the situation, they will move through the process with more comfort and the poser will find a comfortable, albeit somewhat anonymous, hole to fill. If the poser is not comfortable with this new role, he or she could escalate the affect on the team by becoming a disrupter.

Disrupters cause the team to be inefficient. They will do anything to hear themselves speak. Accuracy and precision do not concern disrupters. They have decided their agenda transcends that of the group. Their one goal, consciously or unconsciously, is to do whatever it takes to subjugate the needs of the team to their own plans. The difference between posers and disrupters is that disrupters could care less whether the team succeeds or fails, as long as their strategy is embraced. Disrupters are loud and aggressive. Their arsenal is varied and effective. Their effect is lasting and should be feared. If you have a disrupter on your team, have a one-on-one session behind closed doors. Review your expectations, assess where the disrupter is in relation to the standards you expect, offer your input about how the disrupter can change behavior, and be clear. Make it known that current performance is not in line with the vision you have for the team and then challenge the disrupter to change. When I have disrupters on my team, I find that the key to rehabilitation is discovering what motivates them and then providing that motivation to spur on appropriate actions. One innovative method I use to ferret out this hidden information is that I ASK! Even so, be aware that if you can't get there from here, this is another case where you as the leader may need to exorcise the group by removing the bad actor. Disrupters and posers have a negative effect on the group, to be sure, but in some cases their effects can be devastating.

Sometimes, teams have members who are not comfortable in group situations. Still, they are on the team because they bring value or have critical skills. Two examples of this more submissive behavior are the low talker and the sideliner. This behavior stems from a perceived lack of confidence and is exacerbated by the stress of the situation. It is certainly likely that some on the team will be less vocal than others; that's just the calculus of group communication. Still, I have seen over and over again that these low talkers and sideliners sometimes possess the pearl of knowledge that ends up being the key to the solution to a problem. Through their silence may come clarity: it is just their personal response to the pressure. A leader needs to pull these team members from the sideline and give them a voice. Solicit their input by making the atmosphere comfortable for them. Sometimes, this means speaking to them one-on-one, and at other times, quieting the crowd will suffice. I have found that if you build a space for these team members to speak, they will take advantage of it. Their problem is that they don't have the confidence to assert their ideas within the group discussion and the environment prevents them from contributing. From time to time, this is a result of the inertia that powers the group dynamic in a high-pressure situation.

Inertia worshipers like to go with the flow. They are uncomfortable rocking the boat. They would never roll down the window of their car on the highway and stick their arm out into the air stream! I have been in high-pressure situations where inertia has such a physically powerful hold that the team cannot break free of its effects. This is fine with the inertia worshipers. They like the feeling of being pulled along by the situation. The danger is, obviously, that the situation may be pulling you in the wrong direction. Remember, the goal is to always act on purpose in a high-pressure situation. Sometimes this is counter to the building inertia. Inertia affects perception, communication, and motivation. Someone must "drive the bus." I remember working with a group of financial advisors in Boston in debriefing a meeting with a large client. Several errors were made and confidence was undermined in the meeting. This caused the client to put out a Request for Proposal (RFP) and jeopardized the account. In the debrief, the relationship manager said out loud, "I guess the ball got dropped."

I stopped him immediately. "The ball didn't get dropped; someone dropped the ball." I broke the inertia. If we were going to get to the root cause of the problem, we had to define reality, but inertia pushed us down the track of "we have to be nice to everyone." We absolutely want to work in a favorable, considerate atmosphere—outside of the debrief room. In the debrief, we want to get to the root cause of the issue—and then we leave it in the room. A leader needs to drive the bus and assert control over the situation, rather than letting inertia take control of the situation. Being proactive is the key to weaning the inertia worshipers back into the fold.

Think about how the people you know change in a group situation. Do they morph into any of these types of people we have discussed? Why? Can you add to the list? Do you have a technique to get everyone back on the same page? Go back to the beginning. Who do you want on your team in a high-pressure situation? Here's my wish list:

Passionate team players with a bias for action focused on driving results[16]

Think about it:
Passion = Speed is life
Bias for action focused on driving results = Lose Sight, Lose Fight
Team players = Check Six

Teams have a personality of their own. This is a good thing! Diversity is crucial. I want many different kinds of personalities on my team who can rally around the objective. When I am consulting with a team on a performance issue, I try to frame the discussion in simple terms. Since everyone brings an individual worldview and approved solution to each high-pressure situation, I challenge them all to step back and look at the team from high altitude. We always start with the objective, because that gives the team direction. Does everyone understand the objective? Does everyone understand how his or her role will support the objective? Next, we look at the information available. We must define reality in order to construct a viable plan of action. After that, it is time to get to work. It is critical that team members are sensitive to how each individual reacts to pressure and how the team as a whole reacts. Talk about it. Put it up in lights! Elevate awareness so

---

[16] Port, Michael. *Book Yourself Solid*. John Wiley and Sons, 2006. Defining this is an exercise in this great book.

that these reactions can be dealt with in stride. Pressure impedes progress. Admit it, and move on.

It would be great if you could assemble your dream team every time you are confronted with a high-pressure situation. Do you know who you'd pick and why? If you don't, take a moment and think about it. Write it down and refine it. Remember, it is a wish list, but it will at least give you a VECTOR. As you can see, I'd pick passionate team players with a bias for action focused on driving results. I relate it back to the three axioms of a fighter pilot.

Passion is an accelerant. Passion is a fuel. I love having passionate people on my team. Passion builds confidence and helps me lead in high-pressure situations. When I am surrounded by passionate people, I always feel like, whether I am prepared for a situation or not, we'll figure it out—together. Passion does not have to be loud, nor does it have to be overt. Passion, used effectively, is contagious. Having a team of people who are passionate can be your biggest asset. *Speed Is Life.* When I pick my dream team, I want passionate individuals who I can become focused into an effective team.

Working together effectively is critical in a high-pressure situation. That's why I want team players on my side. How individuals coalesce as a team becomes a force multiplier. The synergistic affects of a team mentality will have an exponential—not linear—effect on the performance of the group. Working together, the team can see around the corner to anticipate, identify, and control the myriad action items contained in a stressful situation. Sometimes, teams "fit" naturally, and sometimes, a leader has to lay the groundwork for the team. No matter the case, the hard work up front by a leader to develop a team mentality pays enormous dividends in a high-pressure situation. Still, if a team doesn't understand the objective and its specific role in producing results, success will prove elusive.

The last component I look for in a team is that they collectively develop a bias for action focused on driving results. I want people "leaning forward," because it encourages every member of the team to be a leader at her or his specific level of responsibility. This is a concept straight out of fighter aviation. When we are on a mission, we always have a flight lead, or someone in charge of the formation, who makes the administrative and tactical decisions, not only for a safe flight, but also for a tactically successful sortie. But within the formation, every wingman is expected to, and must, lead at his level. Tactical leaders are responsible for their own jets, their targeting, and their wingman. Without leaders at every level, the formation will not be able to employ effectively, no matter how insignificant the threat. A seemingly insignificant example of this illustrates my point quite well.

When I was in Operation Southern Watch in 2000, my mission was to enforce the southern no-fly zone south of the 32nd Parallel in Iraq. I'd typically lead out three other F-15s from our base in Saudi Arabia and marshal the entire package, usually upwards of thirty Air Force and Navy jets, just south of the Iraqi border in the Honus Military Operating Area. There, I'd position my formation, refuel with airborne tankers, and work my timing to cross into bad guy land exactly to the second. The F-15s were always the first ones in country, our role being to sweep the area for any enemy fighters so that the rest of the package could enter unimpeded. Each of my three other wingmen had a specific position and role to play. I was the flight lead, so my job was to make sure we were on time and our CAP was in the correct position. Most importantly, I made all of the tactical and administrative decisions for the group. My number two man was the primary weapons delivery platform tactically, but also monitored all of the emergency airfields in case we had to duck into one. My number three was the deputy flight lead. His role was to back up everything I did. Finally, my number four was the secondary enforcer and administratively was in charge of ensuring that the package players were checking in on time. We each had specific roles, all in support of our objective. Back in the Honus MOA, I turned my formation to run to the border. I had played the strong headwinds perfectly and our timing was to the second. An aside here, as a flight lead, one nonverbal indicator of how your formation is handling their work load is their formation positioning. First off, we want to look good, so being in the exact briefed position shows me as the flight lead that my wingmen are handling their tasks and able to update their formation position. Second, I have my wingmen in a specific formation for a very specific tactical reason. If they are out of position, the integrity of the formation can be compromised. Every single time we'd approach the border, I'd see my wingmen start to creep in front of me. They were supposed to fly exactly line abreast and about 1.5 miles apart from me. But as the border crossing into Iraq neared, slowly they'd creep forward. We'd cross the line close enough to provide mutual support, but out of formation position and I knew exactly why. The reason they'd creep forward is they all wanted to be the first ones across the line into bad guy land! Talk about proactive! These are exactly the kinds of people I want on my team!

Passionate team players with a bias for action focused on driving positive results

In business, the same is true. Having a bias for action encourages team members to make decisions in a high-pressure situation rather than to absorb the environment around them. By communicating your expectation to maintain a bias for action, as a leader you are saying, "If you don't know what to do, do something!"

There are obvious caveats to this mentality and it is important that these boundaries are clear as well. Get the momentum going, seek advice, and execute. As a leader, you must provide the framework for your team to make effective decisions. Again, having a clear vision, predictable approaches, and a specific objective is critical. Within these bounds, let your team "take the ball" and run. You don't have time to guide the team through every process or procedure. Empower them with the responsibility to affect the outcome and then debrief them on how they did in relation to the objectives. In a high-pressure situation, you need your team to stay ahead of the situation as much as they can, or they will be buried. Developing a culture of leaders at every level will change the approach to everything you do. Realize, though, if you let your team truly have a bias for action, you are allowing them to potentially make mistakes.

Newsflash: mistakes happen all the time. Mistakes are a leadership laboratory for learning as long as you burrow down to the root cause(s) in a debrief. Fighter pilots even make mistakes! (Copy the sarcasm?) What I have found in the business world is that the difference is that when a fighter pilot makes a mistake; we debrief it, put it up in lights, and learn from it. This group learning process ensures that we learn from each other's mistakes and, hopefully, don't make the same mistakes over again. This is a simple process to ensure constant improvement. Understand and acknowledge that there is a difference between a mistake and a crime. The distinction comes down to intent. If you knowingly break a rule, you may have committed a crime. That needs to be dealt with in a completely different way than a mistake. In a high-pressure situation, a team with a bias for action will surprise itself by turning potential into effective execution. The upside of this mindset will always outweigh the downside of the mistakes made. When your team reaches its full potential, it will have a bias for *purposeful* action focused on driving results.

Teams are an entity onto themselves. Leaders make a mistake when they choose the team using a myopic lens, that is, based solely on the personalities of the members in the team. This is because the team dynamic itself will change the behavior of the individual members. I encourage my clients to populate the team by starting with a clear objective. Then, choose members with appropriate skill sets to achieve that objective.

Finally, lay the groundwork for the team with a clear vision, specific tactical objectives, and defined roles. It is a place to start. Sometimes you won't be able to choose the team to attack a high-pressure situation, and sometimes the team, once together, will take on a personality of its own. That's when you must LEAD! So where do you start? Again, simple! You start by building the culture in which your "wingmen" know that they have the opportunity, resources, and support to be leaders at their own appropriate level.

7

The Foundation:
A High-Performance Culture

"Champions know that success is inevitable."
—Michael Gelb

VII. The Foundation: A High-Performance Culture

As the sun peeked its head just above the horizon on the morning of September 12, 2001, America awoke with a new perspective. I stopped at the Dunkin' Donuts near my house on the way to Otis Air National Guard Base and already I could see people making preparations to overtly display their solidarity with the ideals that made this country great. Flags were hung with care and strength, and the usually rather loutish citizens of Cape Cod were all of the sudden genteel and courteous. In a sense, the somber mood and tragic events of the day before were stripping away the daily, mundane slog. In a way, we were given a gift of clarity as a result. People were reexamining what was truly important in their lives and, for me, the answer was unambiguous: God, family, country.

When I arrived at the squadron, friends, and coworkers had been at it all night. The flight line was a city unto itself, with technicians preparing the jets for whatever tasking awaited. The talk among the Guard members focused on "activation." Most of the citizen soldiers of the Massachusetts Air National Guard served in a part-time capacity. They had other jobs to go to after their military service was completed and worked at Otis one weekend a month and two weeks out of the year. With the significant increase in operational tempo, it was clear that commanders would have to augment the small full-time force. This meant that some of the force would have to be activated, or "called up" to active duty. They'd be asked to leave their civilian employ and assume a full-time position at the base. For some, this included a considerable pay cut, substantial commute times, and disruption of family life. For the pilots flying the missions, they too were in the hot seat.

Most did not care about a possible activation. In fact, pilots from all over the country were calling in from their airline trips to volunteer to fly as soon as they could make their way back to Otis. Commanders on the base carefully considered all of their options and the implications of their decisions. They needed personnel to meet the tasking, but they understood the far-reaching consequences of activating a citizen-airman. In the next few hours, the leadership in the fighter squadron found themselves in a completely different situation. All of the pilots were calling in asking to be tasked. To a pilot, when someone started a sentence with, "Could you...," it was curtly and abruptly interrupted with an affirmative response. We understood how important the next few months would be in the history of our great country and it was time for us to step up. That was our culture. We were proud and honored to serve.

It seems that whenever I bring my techniques and tools to a corporation, no matter where it is in the country, one of the first questions I am asked by the "masses" is, "Does our leadership get this training?"

"Absolutely," I respond emphatically. The training I have developed will not work unless it permeates from the top down. If the leaders of the company are not on board, then the principles I teach can't work. The reason this is the case is because I teach culture change. Without the proper framework, the support necessary to sustain the methodology I bring to business cannot work. It's as simple as that. Moreover, without a culture that puts a premium on leadership at every level, focused on execution, the advanced techniques and tools required to overcome high-stress situations will break down. Culture is a critical element and the culture starts from being defined at the top of the company. The concept with which I begin every engagement is the importance of cultivating what I call a "high-performance culture." In a job where lives are on the line, the culture is the lynchpin for success. The same is true when livelihoods are on the line in business.

Think about these questions: What defines your company's culture? How does the public perceive you? How does your boss see you? Are you comfortable? These are all indicators that I use to gauge the corporate culture. When you are speaking in front of hundreds of people, there are other ways to gain insight into the kind of culture that a company has. For instance, I look at how many people are wearing clothing that identifies them as part of the company (shirts, ties, etc.). Do they talk about their role in the company and the company itself when I meet them? How do they group together socially before the seminar? These are all indicators to me. In the best fighter squadrons I have been assigned to, you can immediately sense the culture of pride and excellence the first day you show up.

When my family and I were assigned to the 53rd Fighter Squadron at Spangdahlem, Germany, I was assigned a sponsor to help me navigate the challenges of moving overseas with a wife, two toddlers, and a dog! I received a welcome package focused on the first two weeks I arrived in country before I even showed up. The package talked about getting from the airport to the base, where to stay on the base, where to eat the first few days, banking, license information, and where to get a car. But it went even further. My sponsor told me that he'd meet me at the airport and that his family would bring me dinner the second night—he had arranged pizza the first night in Germany because our day would not synch up to German time. I felt confident about moving now. Still, there was more. After meeting us at the airport, my sponsor drove us to the temporary housing on the base where an enormous sign was draped on the door. It said, "Welcome to the 53rd Fighter Squadron, Home of the NATO Tigers!!" What a great first impression. When we opened the refrigerator to put our half-full water and baby bottles in, there was no room! The refrigerator was completely stocked by my sponsor, diapers were in the bedroom, and a welcome basket was on the table—along with study guides for the German driver's test that he had scheduled for us to take the following week. When I asked if I could pay him back for his trouble, he said, "No, but when you're a sponsor, do the same thing for the new guy coming in." I had been in the country for about three hours, I knew one person in the squadron, and my family was tired from the long trip, but I knew exactly the kind of culture I was walking into. What does your company do to welcome new employees?

In one very successful Boston financial firm that I consulted with, considered to be a leader in their industry, they simply showed new employees their cubicle, handed them three binders of information, and set them loose. For the next year, it was up to the employee to "figure it out." Imagine the impression the new employee got. Then imagine how much more efficient the employee could be with a one-day orientation. The benefits far outweigh the costs. In the case of this financial firm, the cause and effect were significant in very tangible ways. Of course, there are quality of life issues that are very important, but this approach to "welcoming" a new hire also affected the bottom line. During one of my workshops, I asked the teams to list all of the tools the company provided for them to do their jobs efficiently. They ran the gambit from Microsoft Office to proprietary software that the company developed in-house. Although in this case not one person in the group of approximately 50 people were new hires, there were several programs that a significant percentage present had never used or heard about. One of these "efficiency tools" had been the subject of a company-wide initiative. When I asked who or what group "owned" the program, no one could answer. So here we had a company-sponsored software initiative that a substantial number in the group had never used and no one knew who managed. These are exactly the kinds of issues that can be handled with a simple, straightforward program for new hires. What kind of culture do you want to work within?

Culture change does not happen overnight. *Speed Is Life.* It is a process, which is why it must begin at the top. The culture change we taught at Fighter Associates was based on focus, attitude, communication, training, and support. Since I am a product of years of Air Force training and business experience, there have to be acronyms involved! When Duff and I drilled down to find the true culture of an organization, we assessed their **F**ocus, **A**ttitude, **C**ommunication, **T**raining and **S**upport. FACTS. The focus of the organization or team is a great place to start because most of the time, we found that the team members can be focused like a laser beam if they need to be, but they had not been given anything to be focused on.

When it comes time in the seminar to talk with my clients about focus, I put the vision, goals, and objectives of their own company on the board. Then I ask if anyone has ever seen them? Usually, about 10% know them and another 10% have seen them, but the vast majority of people attending aren't sure. I explain to that group that it's okay because with most of my clients, the numbers break the same way. In the days after the attacks of September 11, 2001, then-President George W. Bush told the military that they had a new objective: to win the war on terror. So what did this mean to me? Did it mean I was supposed to get my gear on, jump in my F-15, takeoff, and win the war on terror? Of course not. I had to figure out what piece of that objective I owned. For me, my piece was to sit alert at Otis, with all that entailed and demanded, and be ready at a moment's notice.

Here's the problem: if you don't know the vision, goals, and objectives of your company, I guarantee your subordinates don't know either. In fact, the danger is that in the absence of a VECTOR for your group, they will search one out which may not be a direction in which you want them to proceed. If your company and department does not have specific, measurable, achievable, realistic, and timely objectives (SMART), then take up the task and get them. Objectives define purpose and hone focus. I challenge my clients to take it one step further and I have them develop objectives for each individual—personal and professional. Here's a good example.

When I was with the Fighter Associates consulting group, one of our largest clients spent hundreds of thousands of dollars to develop their annual goals. They deployed an internal marketing plan to create a buzz and spread the word. At the end of the quarter, they found that many of the relationship managers and their teams were missing the mark. Tim Duffy and I were the project leads with this client and we found out something very interesting.

This company was at the top of their peer group. They were making a lot of money, but brought us in because they were not happy being in the top 10. They wanted to be number one. This year, their objective was to grow business, retain existing clients, and integrate across the company. When Duff and I discussed these objectives with the very enthusiastic vice president of the group, the problem became clear. First of all, I asked if he thought these objectives were Specific, Measurable, Achievable, Relevant and Timely (SMART.) There were enough internal controls and metrics in place to make them measurable. They were a large financial company—give me a break! The numbers were certainly attainable based upon past performance and external environments. They were also well within the relationship manager's reach. In this company, objectives were evaluated and measured quarterly, and they were realistic. The problem Duff and I had with these objectives came down to whether they were specific enough. Duff asked the VP, from the perspective of his team members, what objective was more important: growing his book of business or retaining a client? Fifteen minutes later, I asked whether integration across the company was more important than growing the book. Another 15 minutes. You see, the objectives were fine. Duff and I could tell that the only problem with them was that the leadership had not prioritized them. *Lose Sight, Lose Fight.* This simple step provided the focus relationship that managers needed to take the company to the next level. So, rather than marketing this internally with horizontal visuals, Duff suggested a vertical depiction. When I asked the VP how he would stack it, he said, "Simple: grow, retain then integrate." That was that! Now relationship managers understood in no uncertain terms that their highest priority was to grow their book of business; next, do what it takes to retain clients; and then finally, integrate with other parts of the company. It was no use forcing integration if a relationship manager was losing clients out the bottom of the book! Now the relationship managers knew exactly what to do. Once their mindset had become "maintain a bias for action," if they ever lost momentum, they knew that they should start again by growing their book of business.

Do you have SMART objectives for your team? Are they prioritized? If not, take some time and define the objectives to empower your team to maintain its bias for action and produce the results you need. Objectives define purpose.

Once you have armed your team with prioritized SMART objectives, it is easier for them to understand the piece of the objective which they own. It adds accountability to the process. Accountability and responsibility remind team members of their priorities. As a leader, you must understand that you can delegate responsibility, but you can only share accountability. When you define accountability and responsibility, your team understands the expectation. After that, it is time to expand the meaning and interpretation of focus by prioritizing the SMART objectives that you identified.

Take a look at this picture of my friends Pete "Abner" McCaffrey and Clark "Buck" Rogers. If you've ever been to an air show and seen the U.S. Air Force Aerial Demonstration Team, the Thunderbirds, you've seen this signature move. From the perspective of the person on the ground, the "high-speed pass"

looks as if the two jets that Abner and Buck are flying pass right through each other. They orchestrate this maneuver from each side of show center to arrive in the middle of the crowd's view at exactly at the same time. Abner's responsibility is to fly the precise line and make the timing work out, and Buck's responsibility is to not hit Abner! So, you could say priority number one is don't smash into each other. But let me ask you this: is not hitting each other their only priority? No. It's their *highest* priority right now, but in about one millisecond, they will have put this maneuver behind them and they'll be on to the next, only to be revisited in the debrief. Here are some of their priorities: don't hit each other, don't hit the ground, don't hit anything attached to the ground, plus their timing, radio calls, fuel status, engines...on and on.

If Abner and Buck fly this perfectly and miss each other, but then hit the ground, it won't matter whether they were exactly at show center when they passed. If they nail this maneuver but totally buffoon the next because their timing or ground track was off, no one will remember if the high speed pass was spot on—they'll remember the next maneuver that was not flown with precision. It's the same in business.

There are many goals, objectives, and missions to accomplish in the business day. It is dizzying to think about how many external and internal factors can get you off your game. So, when you're boss says "focus up," what does it mean to you? Focus up can't mean anything unless you understand your objective, know what you are accountable and responsible for, and then prioritize the task that will enable you to achieve that objective.

Now "focus" means something. It is tangible. More importantly, it is something you can execute. Focus also affects the manner in which you execute. This is something fighter pilots do right: execute with attitude. But this concept is not something out of *Top Gun*. Attitude can be the fuel to achieve success, or it can be the distraction that contributes to failure.

General John Jumper, former Chief of Staff of the Air Force, once said, "Pride is the fuel of excellence." Attitude begins with pride. Is your team proud to be working with you? If not, then is your team proud to be working with your company? Pride is the first pillar of attitude. In a high-performance culture, your leadership needs to focus on building pride individually and in the corporation. This certainly is not an exact science and it takes constant maintenance, but if your individuals are not proud to be where they are, it is just a matter of time before a high-pressure situation magnifies problems into something unmanageable. Pride pays incredible dividends not only because it fuels superior performance, but it also helps to define the perception that those outside your team have of you and your wingmen.

Fighter pilots often are type cast into being cocky. It is a mark earned by many unconfident pilots. It is born in the fighter pilot who doesn't quite have the confidence to let his execution speak for itself. You can see it in the pilot that "hot dogs" it in the traffic pattern so everyone can see, but can't execute in the heat of the battle. In the traffic pattern, the unconfident fighter pilot controls the situation to ensure his maneuvers are flown to perfection. In the heat of the battle, it is more difficult to control the high pressure situation. This is where the cocky pilot misses his targeting responsibility, makes an excuse and is defensive about it in the debrief. A confident fighter pilot is completely different.

Confidence comes with experience and hard work. It is a result of a million mistakes that are acknowledged, researched, identified, and worked on. It is completely different from cockiness. The confident fighter pilot uses the fuel of pride to execute on every mission with consistency. No one has to tell him. It certainly does not mean he is flawless, but it does mean that he has developed his skill set to manage the situation, or he asks for help – *Check Six*! How does the public perceive your company? Do they think your team is cocky or confident? Do they even care? Ask your clients! If the answer is not to your expectation, reflect on what exactly defines your corporate culture. If you can't clearly define this, it's okay—you're in good company—but make it your mission to start this process by building on the tenets of a high-performance culture. Make no mistake: culture change takes time, but the good news is that if you have support from the top, it can germinate from any level. Don't wait; *you* start the process by defining how you perceive your competition, your approach to leadership, and the discipline with which you execute your tasks.

In my job flying F-15s, I don't have competition, I have adversaries. Lives are lost if I make a mistake. Maybe your job doesn't hold such clear-cut outcomes, but you do have competition and, most certainly, livelihoods can be lost in your business—not the least of which is YOUR livelihood if you can't produce results. I am not saying that all of your competition needs to be processed as an adversarial relationship, but what I am saying is that when livelihoods are at stake, you'd better be able to execute with the perception that your adversary is going to wish they were you, not the other way around! Take the focus and attitude of a high-performance culture and demonstrate it by being a leader at your level.

Have you ever been to an air show? You and 500,000 of your newest friends waiting in line for $10 hot dog! Well look at this picture of  Thunderbird Abner McCaffrey. Concentrate on the two men by the right wing—the crew chiefs. In this picture, Abner (who is in the cockpit of the F-16) is at the end of runway check, where the two crew chiefs give the jet one last comprehensive check over. Think of the responsibility. They check every inch to ensure that the jet is ready to go fly. If they see anything wrong, they have the responsibility to send Abner back to the chalks. The crew chief is the subject matter expert on all things technical and mechanical. They are accountable because they are leaders at their level. It is an interesting dynamic, because Abner is higher rank, Abner wants to go fly, and Abner is "the Thunderbird!" Think of the pressure. Five hundred thousand people waiting in the hot sun to go see Abner yank and bank around the pattern. Still, these two men are accountable and, because their support system is based upon a high-performance culture, if they see something wrong, their word is not questioned. They have earned that respect. Being a leader at your level doesn't mean that you will make the decisions that the CEO of the company has to make, just as it doesn't mean that these crew chiefs have to make Abner's decisions. It does mean, however, that in a high-performance culture, we demand that everyone lead at their appropriate level and speak out, especially in a high-pressure situation. As a leader, you must cultivate this mindset and provide the training and resources that your people need to be able to achieve this goal. You hired your team members because of the potential and the skill they bring; don't be afraid to give them the chance to succeed. Now, help every leader in your high-performance culture by teaching and demonstrating the hidden force multiplier—discipline.

You could have the best corporate culture in your industry, but if you don't have discipline, it will all be for naught. As I have said before, I teach my clients to strive to keep their emotions in check but still maintain a bias for action. It's a principle I teach called "controlled aggressiveness." When I get a new pilot in the F-15 on my wing and we are going out to fight one-on-one, many times the pilot will not maneuver the jet with the force required to achieve my objectives. It is uncomfortable to sustain action under such heavy g-forces: your body gets sore and you end up panting like you've run a 400 meter sprint. Still, in the heat of the battle, the ability to fly your jet at the edge of the envelope could be the razor-thin difference between life and death. In the debrief, we critique these maneuvers in painstaking detail and the pilot always leaves vowing to do better the next time. The next mission is almost predictable.

Most of the time coming off a mission like this, for the new guy, the next mission is wrought with too much maneuvering, which leads to exceeding the aircraft's capabilities. In these cases, the mission is usually terminated early because the new pilot has over-g'd the jet, or exceeded the allowable g-force load. In their haste to prove themselves worthy, they have been overzealous. Now, the debrief consists of teaching the new pilot that there is a difference between maneuvering in relation to the bandit and being exceedingly harsh with the aircraft controls. The difference is controlled aggressiveness. I tell the new pilot not to just go out and pull on the stick; rather, be as aggressive as needed to defeat the adversary while maneuvering within the limitations of the jet, and then I demonstrate how to do it on the next mission. The same concept applies to business. Use controlled aggressiveness.

On the business battlefield, controlled aggressiveness is a critical tenet of a high-performance culture. It means that just enough time, effort, and resources are expended to meet the adversary, while at the same time understanding the internal and external environments. Sometimes that means pushing the limit (*Speed Is Life*), like when a marquee client sends out a Request for Proposal unexpectedly. Sometimes it means slowing things down (*Speed Is Life*), like when regulatory procedures are called into question. In either case, cultivating a controlled aggressiveness mindset will ensure that your team knows where the line is between meeting the adversary with the appropriate force or pumping the breaks to stay within the guidelines of the values and goals of the organization. Once the mindset has found its way into the culture, the heavy lifting begins with how we interact every minute of the day.

I have a saying with my clients: no matter how many times you send a message out, and no matter what means you use, 10% of your team will never get the word. I use this bit of hyperbole to emphasize that as a leader in a high-performance culture, you need to assume that someone on your team is missing the message. You are simply contingency planning for gaps in communication. In the high-performance culture within which I grew up, we have both an administrative and an operational chain of command. The administrative chain is formal and based on rank. The operational is more esoteric. For instance, if I am the flight lead of a formation of two F-15s, and the wing commander, who happens to be a general and who outranks me, is my wingman, I have authority to lead him into battle. If he makes mistakes, it is my responsibility to debrief him on it, regardless of rank. Now, there are subtleties to this, I admit. There are times when I call him "two" in reference to his formation position, and times when I call him "Sir" in reference to his rank! Still, in formation, I am one and he is two. Obviously the manner in which we have cultivated this relationship is key to our culture. We do this by assigning "call signs" to each member of our team, in a time-honored tradition known as the naming ceremony. We use verbal jousting as a technique to show comfort in our communication. We use these in the squadron to break down the communication barriers that exist because of the administrative structure. How does your high-performance culture empower lower-level leaders to speak?

When I ask this question in my training session, I usually get the same answer: "I have an open-door policy." Great! So what? If your team is afraid of "the boss," do you think they're going to walk through the door? Nope. I offer a different technique. Keep the door open, but use the doorway to leave your office and go out to seek input. Find out about your team members and their families. Find a way to connect. Then, when they are comfortable, go get them and bring them to your office! Sometimes you'll find that the best ideas on ways to improve the operation are hidden just beneath the intimidation your team member harbors. As with any activity, be prepared.

How much time do you spend preparing for a speech to the organization? Do you spend the same amount of time preparing for an information training meeting? My point here is to always prepare to communicate. Be clear and concise and

SCRAMBLED – by Martin Richard

solicit inputs up and down the organization. I cannot tell you how many times I have changed my presentation the night before because the demographic of the audience was not what I thought it would be, or because management wanted to confront a stressful situation late in the planning meeting. Start preparing by understanding your goals for communication and your message. Practice! Bounce ideas off of trusted mentors. Listen for what is being said and what is not being said. Sometimes the things trying to hide under the carpet are screaming the loudest in your company. Be an active listener. Most importantly, always strive to give information as opposed to data. I am sure you have seen all too often the Powerpoint slide crammed with so many bullets that your eye loses focus. That is data. Give your people information. *Lose Sight, Lose Fight.* Translate the data for them and neatly package a take-away that is easily identifiable and understood. In high-pressure situations, we must constantly work to do this in my line of work as a fighter pilot.

For instance, especially in high-pressure situations, I need to get information from my wingman, so I'll call out on the radio for his "status." I am asking my wingman to tell me what he sees on his radar and about his aircraft condition. Many times the call will go unanswered. My wingman hears me; the problem is that he is so task-saturated that he cannot process the data in front of him into information, so he is silent. The other extreme happens when my wingman responds to a "status" call with a never-ending stream of consciousness. He tells me everything he sees on his radar, whether it's a factor or not. He is giving me data. Again, he cannot process the data and make it into information. From a communication standpoint, as a leader, it is time for me to start downloading tasks. Be specific about what you want him to know and the information you need. This will allow him to prioritize tasks to meet the objective. The principles of focus, attitude, and communication should flow into your training program.

In the Air Force, the mantra is "train like you fight," and I teach my clients that this is step two. Step one is to have a training program that equips your team members with the knowledge they need in a way that they not only can understand, but also that enables them to employ it at their desk tomorrow. The hallmark of the training I do is a logical, building-block approach based on a desired outcome. Set training objectives for every training engagement. Typically, when I am featured as a speaker at a corporation's "training," I ask them what their objective is. If they can quantify it at all, it usually comes down to being an experiential event; leaders will say something like, "I want my people to hear your message."

Courtesy prevents me from asking, "Really? What is *your* message?!"

Not a good way to start off our relationship. Rather, I ask them for their current annual, semi-annual, and quarterly objectives. I already know them from the research I have done prior to the meeting. Then I ask about their leadership philosophy and vision. Finally, I ask them to relate to me what they want their people to hear. What I find with almost every speaking engagement I do is that I am just another in a long line of random training events. I insist that my clients start by building a training plan and then I help them by identifying the objective of the training in the first place. In doing so, training expectations and standards will percolate to the surface.

Standards are very important in training because they ensure that team members understand and can execute on the principles taught before moving on to the next step. This building-block approach ensures a logical progression and identifies shortfalls, and fixes them before sending team members to the next training event. Still, in a high-performance culture, team members are taught that they are in charge of their own training. This motivates them to be proactive and gives them the permission to slow down training so that a mastery level can be achieved, rather than just "filling squares." In my experience in business, this can be the edge you need to succeed as an organization, but there will be reluctance by team members. Herein lies the importance of having a high-performance culture. Sure there are limits to how much extra training you can provide. At some point, your team members have to get back to doing the j-o-b. If a team member has reached a plateau in training, there may be a bigger issue than just the training itself.

In cultivating a culture with a bias for action, you are acknowledging that mistakes will be made. Defining the difference between a mistake and a crime is critical when training your team to be leaders, and paramount to building a high-performance culture.

People make mistakes! I am here to tell you—relax—it's okay. In fact, in the business world, mistakes are usually manifest when hard-charging team members try new things, innovate, and push the envelope. Rarely are mistakes some sinister plot to cost the company time and money or to squander resources. How do I know this? I know this because you hire good people. You hire people who want to succeed. You hire people who want to be a part of something special.

When I joined my first Air Force squadron as a brand new fighter pilot, I was described as having "all thrust and no VECTOR." Simply put, my enthusiasm was not reinforced by a commensurate level of experience and direction. My first commander brought me into his office and sat me down. On his desk were strategically placed the aircraft's flying manual and all of the regulations pertaining to flying. He then conveyed his philosophy to me. He said, "There is a difference between a mistake and a crime." He continued by describing my new career as a football game. I was starting on my own twenty-yard line and my goal was to score a touchdown. The sidelines of the field represented the boundaries. If I went outside the boundaries, I was committing a crime. However, in my quest to score a touchdown, he encouraged me to use the entire field. I could roam from side to side and make mistakes, as long as I stayed on the field of play. I cannot tell you how many times I have visualized that playing field in my military and business career. The key for me as the consumer of this newfound knowledge was to understand the difference between a mistake and a crime. It is a simple concept that is rarely internalized in the cutthroat world of business where the perception is that your first mistake could be your last.

In the military understanding, this concept was simple. The regulations formed clear and unambiguous guidelines. If you intentionally broke the regulations, or there was neglect, you were committing a crime. In the business world, it isn't always so easy. Help your team to find and understand where the "sidelines" are. Some will make a career of dancing along the sidelines with the grace of New England Patriots' wide receiver Randy Moss, and others will stumble down the middle of the field. Either is acceptable! Realize that I use the word "crime" in a figurative sense to emphasize the difference. In this context, "crime" doesn't necessarily mean jail time; it does, however, mean that there may be grounds for disciplinary action. Here are some things you can do as a leader to help your team:

1. Define the crimes—Clearly state in writing those company policies that are outside the realm of good conduct.
2. Deal with crimes with consistency—Crimes must be dealt with quickly and consistently. Failure to do so will become a cancer within the organization.
3. Set guidelines—Use formal and informal training sessions to help your team members translate how the policies work on a day-to-day basis so that there is no ambiguity. Chairfly!
4. Have clear standards—During annual and semi-annual feedback sessions, identify the expectations you have for your team and help them be cognizant of times when performance has fallen below the standard.

5. Debrief mistakes—When a mistake is made, take advantage of it! Encourage a no retribution culture in which mistakes are discussed openly and learning occurs so that the mistake will not be repeated.

6. Discuss mistakes—When a mistake occurs, treat it as a learning point and let the lessons permeate the organization.

7. Keep track of them—Keep a record of failures and successes in a continuity book which can function as a resource for the collective corporate knowledge base.

There is a difference between a crime and a mistake. Crimes knowingly and willfully violate company operating policy. This implies intent. Mistakes, on the other hand, are learning points. Your goal as a leader is to cultivate a culture where when a mistake takes place, it is debriefed to standards and group learning occurs. The goal is not to make the mistake a recurring theme. If you push your team to perform to their fullest potential without fear of retribution for mistakes, your organization will discover new and innovative ways to win on the business battlefield and your people will grow. Always make defining the sidelines a part of your training program and give your people the tools they need to execute in a high-pressure situation. Pressure brings ambiguity, but if you train to these standards every time you train, the expectation will become part of the culture and your team will know when and where they stand at all times. Training provides the only substitute for experience. It isn't a perfect substitute, but it is valuable. Fighter pilots are always "chairflying" the next mission. Chairflying is the process of visualizing the entire event from start to finish. It enables us to anticipate pitfalls or areas of concern before they actually happen. We can chairfly in business, too. In fact, when we talk about methodologies, you will see how visualization is imperative, especially in high-pressure situations.

In every training experience, as a leader, seize the opportunity to encourage mentoring and peer support—*Check*

Six! This guides development and fosters growth. It accelerates understanding and provides team members with a support network. In a high-performance culture, it will also push team members to "max perform" in everything they do. Checking each other's six provides a safety net for your team, and that safety net is the last tenet of a high-performance culture—support. Support is critical to mission success. To illustrate, take a look around you. Think about the last success your business unit had. It is easy to identify those members who were on the front lines and brought the win home. Then, I challenge them to dive deeper. I want them to acknowledge those behind the scenes who provided the support for success. Maybe it's the person in finance that distributes the paychecks, or the benefits group that ensures adequate health insurance. Maybe it's the security personnel at the front door or maybe it's the mentor you've had for years. In a high-pressure situation, their role is important, too, because it enables those on the front lines to have peace of mind. Knowing that those details are taken care of enables team members to focus unimpeded. How critical is that?

Imagine providing the kind of support you get on the job all of the time - even when you are off the job. That is what a high-performance culture demands. If your culture does not allow this level of support yet, be the first to set this standard—be the example. Grab your friends' keys when they are having a drink after work. Lend an ear when your team members are having a bad day. Most importantly, be someone who people can count on in high-pressure situations. That is *checking six!* Whether your team members provide direct or indirect support to the overall objectives, as a leader, ensure that everyone knows that each person's contributions are critical to mission success. The key is letting team members know that they have a stake in the outcome. Once this becomes a part of your high-performance culture, they will do magnificent things for you, your team, and the company. It is the best way to build loyalty.

What are you doing to cultivate a high-performance culture? Believe it or not, it can begin with you! Be an example of how focus can define your purpose on the team. Bring some attitude to your daily tasks. Prepare to communicate and acknowledge that not everyone translates your message the same way, nor does everyone get the word in the fog and friction of business battle. Provide your team members with the training they need to succeed in a logical, building-block approach. Teach the difference between a mistake and a crime. Finally, give your team the resources and support it needs to execute under the most stressful situations. Focus, attitude, communication, training, and support equal a high-performance culture. Without a culture to support operations under stress, you cannot deploy a methodology to execute under pressure. And let's face it: in the end, it all comes down to producing results. Does your team spend most of its time putting out fires in a high-pressure situation, or in any situation? Does your team have a process to execute specifically tailored to stressful times? The answer should be "affirmative!" If it is something less definitive, let me share with you a simple method that I developed to ensure anyone, yes, anyone can lead and succeed under the most pressure packed situations—the ACE Methodology. Think about your initial reactions when confronted with a high-pressure situation. Do you react to every pressure-packed challenge in the same way? Do you take a moment to plan, or do you jump right into execution? What if I told you I knew three simple steps that you can do that are universally applicable to any high-pressure situation and that if you followed these steps, you could dominate any stressful environment? Wouldn't you want to give it a try? Indulge me!

The scene in New York City when I arrived on station.
-from scribd.com

8

The Engine:
ACE Methodology

"Becoming a fighter **ACE** is the pinnacle of aviation. No other accomplishment represents a pilot's complete control under the most stressful combat situations in the face of the most absolute consequences."

—Colonel Donald Strout

VIII. The Engine: ACE Methodology

Shortly after September 11, 2001, the Federal Aviation Administration, along with the President, decided it was time to get the public flying again. It was my day to be on "alert," and I anticipated a busy day. In the interest of proactiveness, our unit had more spare jets available than normal. They were prepped and ready to go at a moment's notice. We also had two pilots on a medium response and two more on a longer response requirement. Today, we scurried about the squadron cleaning and arranging because the Commander of the Air National Guard, the highest ranking officer in the Guard, was paying us a visit. He wanted to add his praise to the chorus we'd been hearing for days now.[17]

In the Command Post, Otis Tower notified the entourage waiting to greet the general that his plane was on the ramp. My wingman Wod and I were playing the game and had all of our flying gear on. We watched Fox News with disengaged interest because the St. Louis airport had been evacuated. Apparently, there was reason to believe someone whom authorities were watching had been in the airport. Still, this did not register with Wod and I until moments later.

Typically, we'd only be wearing our g-suits and have the rest propositioned by the jets in case we got SCRAMBLED. We made our way to the Intelligence Division where Lieutenant Colonel Tony "Big Daddy" Mattera was practicing the briefing he was to give to the General. Just then someone from the

---

[17] [The following is an editorial comment!] Unfortunately for us and the country, a scant four years later, the unit would fall victim to the illogical decision of the Base Realignment and Closure Committee (BRAC) and lose its jets. It was the end of an era where the 102 Fighter Wing had supported combat operations all over the world. It had the BEST safety record of any Air National Guard Fighter Unit, was THE corporate knowledge for the Alert mission for 35 years and had garnered an incredible 4 OUTSTANDING Alert Forces Evaluations in a row (a feat never matched before by any unit and probably will never be surpassed.)

command post came running down the hall: "The SCRAMBLE phone is going off!"

I ran down the hall like an NFL halfback as people hit the walls to get out of the way. Wod was right behind me as we jumped into the Alert truck. It was already running and the doors were open. Dennis "Doogie" Doonan waited at the wheel and said, "Let's go!"

As he sped by the general at a high rate of speed, the welcome party looked with concern. I thought to myself that the general must have been skeptical about this SCRAMBLE. Did he think we had orchestrated the whole thing for show? I quickly put that out of my cranium when the hand-held radio barked at me.

"Slam 1, SCRAMBLE 2."

I responded, "Copy, Slam 1, SCRAMBLE 2, authenticate Charlie, Mike, Alpha..."

"November," and off we went.

The first thing I had to do was to complete all of the preflight checks and procedures flawlessly. While the real threat was the TWA jet that we were being asked to intercept, I couldn't get past the fact that I knew that the bigwigs were watching. Once I had acknowledged that, it was time to lend some control to the situation. I jumped into my jet and checked the systems, while the command post read off the target information: it seems this TWA jet from St. Louis, flying to Boston, had a passenger aboard on the "watch list." Now it became clear why the thousands of passengers at St. Louis airport had been cleared from the terminals. My plan was already set and in my mind, I was going over contingencies. I took a second to plan, if even just the most cursory parts of the mission. I knew it would be a very short flight to Boston, so my immediate concern was the traffic in the area.

Three minutes later, I was airborne, climbing to ten thousand feet. It was time to deliver. I thought to myself that there was no way Wod was going to be able to hang on, but when I looked out the left side of the aircraft, he was in perfect position!

I asked the Boston approach controller for the position of the TWA jet and he directed me to a conga line of jets on final approach to the southwest runways. The line was easy to find, but at 10,000 feet, I could not decipher which one was the target.

"Slam 1, FENCE checks, arm safe, tapes on, CMDs on."[18]

"Slam 2," Wod acknowledged and complied.

I told our NEADS controller that we needed a lower altitude. One reason we needed to get lower was for visibility and the other was because the "look angle" of the radar was reaching its limit. Being so high above the target stretched the limitations of the antenna in the F-15 and we risked losing the target. NEADS responded, "Working it."

I knew immediately that this was a mistake and I would have to debrief myself on this error after the mission. There was no way we were going to receive a lower altitude in time. I called Boston Approach directly and told them that we were going lower. The controller said, "Cleared."

Less than five minutes later, we were flying covertly behind the TWA jet. On the runway at Logan in Boston, emergency services gathered on the edge of the runway. As soon as the plane touched down, they were off to greet it, as well as the suspected terrorist. Thirteen minutes earlier, Wod and I were in the Intelligence Division whining about being a "rent a crowd" for the general's dog and pony show. How quickly things change! Another quiet day interrupted by a high pressure situation.

*   *   *

---

[18] FENCE is an acronym we use to ready all of our combat systems and our CMD's are the chaff and flares we have on board. I wanted to have our flares ready to expend in case the jet was unresponsive after its interception.

The scenario is universal. Your perfectly efficient day is planned down to the minute. In your mind, by organizing and prioritizing the tasks in front of you, success is all but a foregone conclusion. Time passes at a manageable pace as you assemble the resources you need to get the job done. Suddenly, the phone rings. You recognize the caller ID as one of your most profitable relationships. He is deeply concerned. An error in execution has caused your client to be financially vulnerable in a major transaction. After your client explains in painstaking detail what he would like to do with the company you represent, it is clear that a high-pressure situation has found you. It is time to act, but what do you do? You do not have all of the information you need to rectify the situation. The risk of making the wrong decision is daunting. Your thoughts are *SCRAMBLED* and time is passing you by. Ordered plans that you so meticulously prepared give way to chaotic inaction. The situation is not waiting for you; it is taking on a life of its own. Distractions mount. Random thoughts swirl around about who to blame, getting your story straight for your boss, and how you are going to wedge in time for your other "most important" client later in the day. You want to act, but you are paralyzed. The piercing resonance of the dial tone coerces you reluctantly back to reality. You whisper, "This isn't good."

Experience shows that inaction during a high-pressure situation guarantees defeat. More obscure but equally vital is this simple precept: "even a poor plan executed well is better than no plan at all." This principle speaks to the critical importance of having the right people in the right positions at every level of your organization. It illustrates how building a high-performance culture based on focus, attitude, communication, training, and support will result in high-performance execution. *Speed Is Life!*

I am reminded of my very first emergency procedures simulator evaluation as a young pilot. The emergency procedures simulator was the most stressful, painful, and gut-wrenching experience a pilot trainee endures. Although lost on us at the time, the benefit of mastering every conceivable emergency that a jet could muster in a controlled, benign, and sterile environment provided us with the confidence we needed to progress in the program. Most importantly, WE WERE ON THE GROUND IN A SIMULATOR! We couldn't hurt anything or be hurt. Interestingly, the effects of the almost insurmountable stress, coupled with the incredible fidelity of the simulation, often tricked us into forgetting that we were on terra firma. It was all about preparation and execution. Could I as a "trainee" put all that training and knowledge into action under extreme conditions? Could I execute under pressure?

Yet with all of the techniques, tips, and procedures that my instructors imparted, one has stuck with me in peacetime, in combat, and in business: when confronted with a high-stress situation, the first thing you should do is "hack the clock and take a deep breath!" This was a proven technique that I learned while sweating in the simulator. When a pilot "hacks" the clock, he starts the second hand in motion. Taking a deep breath is a calming exercise and allows a pilot to collect his thoughts. Do these actions take care of the problem? No, but together they are illustrative of a mindset. Many times in a high-pressure situation, your first instinct is to fix the problem. In doing so, the danger is that you can make the problem worse. *Lose Sight, Lose Fight!* Hack the clock and take a deep breath. You are taking deliberate action, but you are also controlling yourself so that you can control the situation. The next step is simple: *EXECUTE.* In this situation, gain control by employing ACE with rigid flexibility and controlled aggressiveness—together as a team *(Check Six!)*:

1. **A**bate the threat.

2. **C**ontrol the situation.

3. **E**valuate follow-on actions and **EXECUTE.**

Step 1: Abate or neutralize the threat.

Starting here enables you to take decisive and appropriate action as well as to build a buffer to prevent you from overreacting. Your goal is simple: stop the bleeding. Recognize the high-pressure situation, gather information, seek advice, and acknowledge what the "threat" really is. Do what it takes to ensure that the issue is neutralized.

A high-pressure situation found us on September 11, 2001. It had all of the telltale characteristics, although I actually developed ACE as a result of several high-pressure business engagements. I knew that success hinged on my completing the first step in the process—abating the threat. We had to stop the attack in order to gain control of the situation and set up a DCA CAP. Setting up a combat air patrol within 25 miles of Manhattan ensured our presence over the city at all times. This negated the threat or, literally, stopped the bleeding. The terrorists had won an important battle, but we were beginning to reverse the momentum by neutralizing the threat. Now it was time to establish control. A couple of years later, as I sat behind my desk as regional director for one of the largest corporations in the world, I had no idea that a normal, mundane phone call from an old friend would end with the onslaught of another high-pressure situation.[19]

Doug Smith was a talented leader in a large, west-coast-based home building company. He learned his leadership lessons on the "fields of friendly strife," as General Douglass Macarthur described them when he was professional football player. I was indebted to him for the insight he provided my first leadership training and consulting company, Fighter Associates, as we honed the message that we developed for the business world. It was Doug who believed in our vision enough to give us our first

---

[19] The following is adapted to protect the people involved!

paying job as consultants! As my cell phone vibrated wildly, I flipped it open knowing it was my business partner, Duff.

"Doug Smith just called me, let's talk about a situation he's dealing with right now."

"Sounds, good," I said. I sat back in my chair and prepared my thoughts. He began to tell me about one of Doug's star performers and how a problem had developed with an extremely valuable client. Duff explained that Doug's perfectly planned day had come to a screeching halt when one of his program managers (PMs) sat down in his office, distraught. Doug had called her in to discuss why a previously fastidiously punctual client had started to miss some invoices. After several minutes of small talk and discussion, Doug got the impression there was no obvious answer and made plans to make an onsite visit. Doug's PM fidgeted in her seat. She seemed abnormally intimidated by this benign meeting. "Let's clear up the situation," Doug said as he picked up the phone.

"You can't call them." Doug set the phone down, a bit puzzled. That was the trigger. He felt the utterly familiar twinge of an impending high-pressure situation.

"Why can't I call them?" Doug said. "The problem is not with the client. It is all my fault," his account manager whispered grudgingly.

For some months now, Doug was trying to reconcile soaring customer satisfaction feedback, but abnormally late payments for service, with a historically "good paying" client. Uncharacteristically, this client had developed a disquieting trend of missing the terms of payment laid out in the proscribed agreement. Oh, and of course, it was the biggest client on his Profit and Loss statement (P&L). Doug had enlisted the full complement of resources to help find the root cause of the problem, but to this point, efforts were fruitless. What Doug did not know was that he was looking in the wrong direction. He assumed that it couldn't be a problem with his PM, not in his high-performance culture! Bewildered, he recounted calling in the account manager in charge of this lucrative account.

"What do you mean it is all 'my fault'," he asked.

"Well, I got behind…and there was pressure…and…" the words trailed off into oblivion. She sounded confused. As he listened intently, he fought the urge to imagine his young son in the seat trying with great fervor to explain away a lie. The bottom line was that for various reasons, the account manager had never delivered the invoices in question for payment to the client. The diatribe ended when his account manager said, "I will quit right now if you want me to, or you can fire me. I completely understand." Doug was floored. This was one of his star players. What was she thinking? What was the logic chain? How did this happen? Now, in complete survival mode, he said, "Oh, no, you're not getting off that easily."

At that moment, being in a high-pressure situation, Doug's first and only task at this point was to abate the threat. The task seemed insurmountable, but having a clear objective helped manage the picture in front of him. With an atypical amount of little confidence, Doug had called Duff and asked, "What is my next step?"

"Doug, you have to stop the bleeding," Duff said. "You have to open the lines of communication and identify the problem."

Among the many things that Doug had done flawlessly to this point was that he had refused to let emotion into the conversation. If he wanted to remedy the situation, he knew he could not get emotional. This was a savvy move.

Often, in our business experience, Duff and I have drawn on the leadership lessons we learned in preparing for combat as a fighter pilots, but one thing resonated clearly: business is business and combat is combat. The key to correcting this error in execution was to leverage the relationship he had spent years developing with the client. In point of fact, it was the only way to stop the bleeding. In the administrative structure of the military, "rank" belies the need to leverage relationships for the most part; in business, relationships are vital. The two are similar, but different and distinct. Doug had experienced this firsthand in his football experience. In challenging times, each member of the team had to depend on every other member to get the job done. To be successful, no one player could fulfill every role—it was about the relationship of the team. Firing the account manager would be an emotional response that would only serve to escalate the problem. Future employment was an issue to be dealt with later. "Abate the problem," I said to Duff—that was Doug's first objective.

Information and communication being critical, I asked Duff if Doug had informed his leadership. He had already taken that step. Reluctantly, he briefed his boss on what exactly had transpired. It was not the highlight of his boss's day. Next, I recommended that he set out to inform everyone involved with this high-pressure situation what exactly was going on. Doug's division was in danger of losing several hundreds of thousands of dollars and he had to ensure that everyone was "on the "same page." Having done that, now came the hard part: it was time to define reality.

Together with the account manager, Duff challenged Doug to survey the landscape with respect to this client. This was Duff's sweet spot. He told Doug to consider his division's exposure in strict legal terms. It turned out that the agreement with this client stipulated that if services were not billed within a nominal time period, the client was not necessarily obligated to pay. As he told Duff this, we could imagine his physiological response to this stressful situation—his stomach turned. I told him to hack the clock and take a deep breath and he laughed; he had been in one of my seminars. I could tell it helped. Doug knew that walking in with a stack of invoices would not cut it. Somehow, if he was going to be able to recover any revenue at all, he needed to fashion a plan that would provide the client some perceived value. After all, it wasn't the client's error. Duff reminded Doug that he had not yet fully abated the threat, and exerting control by creating this plan was a fight for another day. We tried to force him to stay focused.

Given that this was one of his best clients, Duff knew from experience that the key to neutralizing the threat was to trust in the existing relationship. At this point, it was the only way to stop the bleeding. The client had invested years in cultivating a relationship with the PM, and firing her would hurt the relationship, so that was off the table for now. She was the corporate knowledge. It also would help Doug define the reality in front of him because she was the only one who knew what the reality was. Trust issues aside, keeping the PM was the only option. The first and only step to allay potential questions was to admit the mistake. In acknowledging the error, Doug was playing to his strongest suit and performing maintenance on the potential looming damage caused. Spotlighting the strong relationship that he had built over the years would pay dividends when Doug moved on to the next phase of action— exerting control. It was time for Doug to schedule a meeting with the client.

Over the next few hours, Doug worked with the client and the account manager to gather all the information needed. When appropriate, he sought guidance from legal, finance, and his boss. This kept the lines of communication open and provided much needed insight.

Doug felt overwhelmed by the task in front of him, so he tried to scope it in manageable terms. He created a plan to present to the client with one objective regarding this high-pressure situation, focused on neutralizing the threat. It started with admitting the error and it put a Band-Aid on the wound.

By neutralizing the threat, you have bought some time. Use this time to try to exert some control over the situation. Granted, in high-pressure situations, control is a relative term, but look for opportunities to drive the action. This may be as simple as setting a specific, measurable, attainable, and timely objective. It may be as complex as formulating a comprehensive contingency plan to deal with the problem. Don't get greedy here. The goal in controlling the situation is to have some effect in shaping the outcome, no matter how small. Doug, Duff and I were pleased with our start, but we understood that the difficult parts of this problem were still in front of us. In my mind, I wandered back to a situation on 9/11.

"Bogey, bullseye 325, 25, fastmover down the Hudson," the NEADS controller said insistently. It was time to execute. He was telling me that an unidentified aircraft was flying southbound over the Hudson and was 25 miles north of the city. This got my attention because it was the same profile that the other two hijacked aircraft used to find their targets. I dropped to treetop level over the city that never sleeps and sped quickly towards the George Washington Bridge. "Identify, divert," the controller set my task and made clear what I needed to do to **a**bate the threat. I locked my radar to the unknown track and looked through my heads-up display to find the jet in question. I wished I could just dial in the correct radio frequency, speak with the bogey, and abate the situation. But, in the absence of any means of communication, I would have to use speed to close the distance and identify the unidentified aircraft. I "gently" coaxed the jet in question out of the area and in so doing had exercised some **c**ontrol over the situation. I provided the stimulus by rejoining on him, rocking my wings to say, "You have been intercepted; follow me." I waited and anticipated the options that the bogey had. He gave me the response I was looking for when he rocked his wings back at me to acknowledge and turned away. I was **e**xecuting my game plan.

In business, having an effect on the outcome may mean that you must first confront perceptions. For another very large home builder on the West Coast, (one of Doug's competitors oddly enough) getting perception under control was the key factor in shaping the outcome of their business problem.

In prosperous times, this company had firmly inserted itself at the pinnacle of the home building industry. Today, with over 100,000 new homes built, it is recognized as one of the nation's largest and most respected home builders. Their pride is apparent in every nail they drive, piece of land they acquire, or home they close. Along the way, in the tumultuous home building market, they have found themselves in innumerable high-pressure situations. Even so, this company took it all in stride. They became masters at abating the countless threats in front of them and the swiftly changing landscape.

In 2004, this builder was at the top of its game. Demand far outpaced supply, driving prices through the roof. The company managed with precision the delicate balance between unprecedented growth and lofty quality standards. They were the king of the jungle. So, as high-fives were thrown across the boardroom table at the end of 2004, sobering news came. It seemed that the results of surveys given to new home buyers had fallen far below expectations. Bewildered, leaders at the company knew they had to deal with this high-pressure problem.

Fully 25% of the sales at this company were due to positive referrals. This enormous number seemingly outpaced that of all the competitors and was a testament to the home buyers' experiences in the process. It was a source of immense pride—and rightfully so. It was also a source of immense revenue. The threat was simple: based upon poor feedback from the surveys, referrals could fall off. Effective steps were taken to abate the threat when a tiger team interfaced with customers for firsthand information to define reality. Now it was time to exercise control.

In working with this home builder, it was apparent that the low survey scores had caught them off guard. They asked Duff and I to help. We asked them to describe the process around the survey system. It seems that the procedure revolved around a series of questionnaires that new home buyers would complete. They were given the surveys in three phases, beginning the day they moved in, then six months later, and finally nine months later. The existing process meant that the data was not compiled and sent back until almost a year later—a

YEAR later! So much had changed in that year that the data was all but invalidated. In working with their talented team, we identified that the root cause of the problem came down to perception.

When I asked them why they were blindsided by the survey results, they said that the results did not mirror the success of the company. When they would build a home, say one of their signature $500,000 residences, they had a perfect record of delivering it on time, providing more value than their competitors, and with fewer than the industry-standard defects. I smiled. I knew exactly what the problem was. Being a home buyer, not a home builder, gave me the insight I needed to help. Duff translated for them!

First of all, he explained that to the buyer, the home did not cost $500,000; it cost HALF-A-MILLION DOLLARS! Second, he described, that from his perspective, he produced his check on time, so why should the company get extra credit for producing the home "on time"—after all, that was the deal, right? Last, he clarified the fact that if he bought a HALF-A-MILLION DOLLAR home; he, as the buyer, didn't expect ANYTHING to be wrong with it, so "fewer than the industry-standard defects" meant nothing from his perspective! As a home buyer, Duff brought a different expectation to this engagement.

Once we had dealt with the challenge of perception head-on and abated the threat, it was easy to exercise control over this high-pressure situation. Dealing with perception is tricky. You have to be aware of your client's worldview (right or wrong) and then fashion an approach to business that makes sense to them. In the case of this large home builder, controlling the situation meant that they would have to go to work to educate the buyer at every step of the buying process. This would serve to set an appropriate level of expectation and help shape buyers' perceptions. More importantly, it allowed them to control the outcome.

The first thing the company did was to start speaking in terms of the buyer's money. A consumer wants to be assured they are getting a great value for the investment they are making. The HALF-A-MILLION dollar home became the HALF-A-MILLION dollar home. Next, I suggested the extra attention to detail that this company's team put into the building process be lauded during the "walk-through" inspections early on in the process. Where the company went beyond code and further than the competition, it was celebrated. The person doing the walk-through inspection would put this up in lights, not keep it a secret. Finally, Duff told company representatives to "level-set" customer's expectations by explaining the process by which imperfections were handled. They introduced the buyer to the warrantee manager that the buyer would be working with to begin building a relationship. This modification in the process benefited both the company and the buyer. Then, they developed a nominal timetable based upon the component in question for when a problem would be rectified. For instance, if there was a problem with a dishwasher, they developed a process by which a new dishwasher would be installed within a week. If a custom front door was the problem, the buyer would be educated that this process was far more intricate and a replacement door would take up to six months to be installed. Buyers were not unreasonable; they just had no frame of reference. The results were amazing.

Six short months later, survey numbers reflected how well the company was doing. Most importantly, the new approach to perception even gave a bump to the percentage of referrals converted into home sales. It also had some positive unintended effects. The sales force had more ammunition to persuade potential buyers. The warranty team got the chance to meet clients in a positive environment rather than on the first disgruntled service call. In dealing with perception, this company was able to exercise control over the situation and shape the outcome. Experience like this helps leaders to sustain their confidence in high-pressure situations.

Doug Smith drew on experiences like this in his dilemma over the missing invoices. With his account manager in the lead, he walked into his client presentation with the sobering task of admitting a colossal blunder and attempting to recover hundreds of thousands of dollars in lost revenue.

Doug started, "I'm here today because we've made a mistake and my objective is to resolve it to keep you as a client, regroup my team and build on this adversity in order to be stronger on the other end."

Once he defined the objectives of the meeting, he felt a twinge of confidence emerge. Based on the client's initial feedback, and by admitting the error (informing all of the parties involved and presenting the actual state of affairs), Doug courageously attempted to delicately exert control. It was not realistic to think the client would accept the stack of invoices that he had just dumped on their desk with enthusiasm. Still, there was a strong relationship between the two. The client knew that the work had been accomplished and that no invoices had been delivered. While they were within their legal rights to ignore the outstanding invoices, they too had a stake in the future of the relationship. Coincidentally, a new agreement was in the works. Doug saw this as his opportunity. In assembling this new contract, he offered to "help" the client by fashioning a payment plan imbedded within the language of the new agreement for the outstanding invoices. It would be completely aboveboard and it would help the client smooth out the payment responsibility; it was also his only chance of recovering the revenue due. He explained in painstaking detail exactly the terms of the agreement and answered the client's probing questions. He resolved not to end the discussion until they were completely satisfied as to the efficacy of the agreement. When they signed, Doug had achieved his second objective: he had exerted some control over the situation.

The day that Doug called Duff and explained the details of his high-pressure event, we gave him about a 10% chance of ever seeing any of the lost revenue, but in the end he recovered over 70%. Now those are results! By abating the threat, Doug strengthened the relationship and took care of the problem. By focusing on the relationship and the new agreement, he was able to exert control and help shape the outcome. Duff and I had provided solid mutual support. In the final analysis, using the ACE allowed us to help Doug take a lost situation and transform it into a winner for his company (in relative terms). Now it was time to follow through and execute. I told Doug, now that he had the first sign of control, that he should take the time to evaluate the current situation to help clarify his next steps.

Control is not a panacea, but it does provide an opportunity to change the look and feel of the circumstances. Careful, timely, and honest evaluation is the key to being able to turn a fiasco into a net gain. The goal here is to capitalize on the tactical action plan and take advantage of opportunities it has created. When the control you exercise has positive results for you, your client, or your challenge, it is time to evaluate what comes next and *EXECUTE*.

Evaluate the effect your action has produced by asking yourself, "Am I winning, equal, or losing?" If you perceive that the situation is getting out of control, believe your perception! You are losing. In this case, be ready to regress back to reforming your approach to the control piece, or even go all the way back to neutralizing the threat. It is likely that if you are losing, you never really fully neutralized the threat or that the action you applied in an effort to exert control was not suitable. If what you are doing is working, but the outcome is still in doubt, you are "equal." In an "equal" situation, it is far better to sustain the existing action than to try to capitalize too soon. If all you can do is neutralize the threat, then keep neutralizing the threat. If you have worked yourself into an equal state, at least you are not losing! In the best case scenario, you have abated the threat, applied a course of action, and it is producing positive results. In this case, you are "winning." Carpe Diem! Seize the opportunity that your actions have created. Follow through by executing. All of the lessons that you learned are worthless if you keep them a secret! The adept manner in which you handled this high-stress situation will resonate with your clients.

A high-pressure situation lends itself to a simple approach if the goal is success. The ACE methodology is employed to combat high-stress situations in a linear approach based upon *ACTION*. The other critical component of ACE tactics is that it prevents losing control during periods of regression. No team is skilled enough to consistently execute with flawless results, especially in a high-stress environment. That's okay! For a process to work under the rigors of extreme stress, it must account for mistakes. ACE tactics do this. If you attempt to exert control and the outcome is negative, you have experienced regression. You must immediately give some ground and regroup by going back to step 1—Abate the threat. If you are deliberate about neutralizing the threat, progression to control will occur quickly. Failure to abate will dilute and obscure the threat and cause inappropriate action. Aligning action with perception and expectation is the key to turning a high-stress situation into an opportunity to grow. This theme drove me to develop this process that I have shared with the biggest corporations in America. More on that later!

My clients employ ACE to meet any high-pressure situations with overwhelmingly positive results, both professionally and personally. Once teams are comfortable with ACE applied to high-pressure situations, they feel empowered to create positive business outcomes from previously random pressure-packed chaotic events. Armed with these tactics, experience has shown that teams are truly able to "ACE" the high-pressure situation and capitalize on it! The next step is building a high-performance culture with leaders at every level of the organization. Cultivating a high-performance culture, coupled with the process framework that ACE tactics provides, results in high-performance execution and drives results for your organization.

ACE is a simple process to deal with an unexpected high-pressure situation. By executing its three steps in progression, anyone can perform under stress. I have found that in business, some high-pressure situations don't smack you in the face and say, "Here's Johnny!"[20] Some high-pressure situations build over a period of time. As a leader, you can sense their presence and it is imperative you act. If you cannot perceive what problem to "abate," then you can't execute ACE. In these cases, there is time to plan. There isn't a lot of time to plan, but there is time to plan. For this situation, I have spent years refining a planning process which produces tangible outcomes from which to choose. The objective is to leverage ANY time you have for planning in a clean, methodical way so that your supervisors can make an informed decision upon which to act. This process is called VECTOR.

On September 11, 2001, a high-pressure situation smacked us in the face (time to use ACE). Preparing for the aftermath, Operation Noble Eagle was as incredibly stressful at times, but by the nature of the mission, it allowed time for careful, purposeful planning—it required a VECTOR.

---

[20] Jack Nicholson, in *"The Shining,* by Stephen King! Wicked scary!

1. **A**bate the threat.

2. **C**ontrol the situation.

3. **E**valuate follow-on actions and **EXECUTE.**

9

The Process:
VECTOR Planning

"The will to win is not nearly as important as the will to prepare."
—Juma Ikangaa, World Champion Marathon Racer

IX. The Process: VECTOR Planning

In the aftermath of September 11, 2001, President George W. Bush asked to address the United Nations. This was as pragmatic as it was symbolic, and I was to lead the formation of four F-15s that circled above during the speech. The objective was straightforward. The FAA had cleared the airspace and we owned the sky above the UN. Still, this mission had a bit more stress involved than the norm. As we readied our plan and discussed tactics, refueling, and contingencies, the phone in the Command Post rang. First, the Secret Service wanted to speak with me. They had their own plan about where to position us to fit within their big picture of security. After several minutes of back and forth, I convinced them to let me drive the best tactics in the air to achieve the objective. Since I had slightly more time in the front seat of the F-15, they reluctantly agreed to my plan. Next, the New York police called. They had devised their own plan for where we should be in the skies above the city. Again, I explained our tactics and asked their indulgence. We agreed that I'd leave the ground plan to them if they'd leave the air plan to me. Next, the office of the White House called. They had a plan for how I should position my F-15s. Once again, I assured them that we'd be where we needed to be to achieve the objective, and asked them to let me have the latitude of developing my own plan. This went on for about an hour. Obviously, from the responses I heard on the other end of the phone, triggers for a high-pressure situation were popping all over the place! Experiences like this, when the pressure is building quickly but when there is still time to develop a comprehensive planning process, is where VECTOR is so valuable.

The ACE process is a simple tool that I developed to help teams move with agility within the context of a high-pressure situation. The goal is to be out in front of the factors causing stress, and is distinctively functional because it helps teams to prioritize, on an operational level, the tasks needed to achieve a tactical outcome. As a planning tool, VECTOR is the next step. VECTOR also overlays an indiscriminate method to focus the team. In other words, it works in any high-pressure situation regardless of the circumstances, time line, or risk level. ACE allows you to have agility on the business battlefield front lines since it is a process solely based upon execution. VECTOR is a step beyond.

VECTOR is a process that lives alongside your normal business planning methodology, but lays in wait as a support function. I developed VECTOR because I saw most companies with whom I worked take copious amounts of pride in describing to me their annual, semi-annual, and quarterly business planning meetings, but when I asked them how they handled business challenges or opportunities that present themselves outside of these formal meetings, there was no clear answer. In my experience, companies handled these out-of-cycle issues by ignoring them. The result was they left money on the table, because they hope their teams were gifted enough to operate autonomously on their own VECTORs to handle the problem. This produces very inefficient, inconsistent, and spurious results. VECTOR gives teams a process. VECTOR ensures that businesses have a formal means to capitalize on opportunities requiring swift, purposeful action outside of the normal business planning cycles. VECTOR works for any company, industry, or lifestyle. The distinction between ACE and VECTOR is that ACE focuses on execution and VECTOR focuses on planning.

VECTOR is a planning cycle tailored for the business world. It is a place to start. *Speed Is Life.* I describe it to my clients as being a tool born from business with a hint of fighter pilot attitude! In aviation, success comes from a linear methodology to ensure safe, effective operations. This methodology is based on a four-step process: Plan, Brief, Execute, and Debrief. Our missions in fighter aviation are constructed around this methodology for a simple reason: what we do is dangerous and expensive. This process ensures that we come back alive and that we get every ounce of training every time we go flying. To that end, in the F-15 community, typically we plan the day before a mission, we brief two hours before the mission, we fly the mission videotaping every aspect of execution, and then we debrief for as long as it takes to find the lessons learned and get better each time. It is a clean process that we complete for every flight, even in combat, but it doesn't cleanly translate to the business world.

In business, I certainly use the Plan, Brief, Execute and Debrief methodology in certain situations, but those who claim that this process fits every business every time are simply wrong. If a business can fit its execution around this methodology, just like we plan our fighter missions around this process, then, of course, it will work. But what I find with my clients is that this only has a limited success and only in the normal planning cycle of operations. Think about it: in business, you don't know where or when the threat or the opportunity is coming from. It was the same on September 11, 2001. These threats and opportunities don't consult your company so that they arrive on your terms! The environment changes and client's needs evolve outside of YOUR planning cycles. Imagine that! *Lose Sight, Lose Fight.* My clients have processes operating within other process, simultaneously, in parallel, perpendicular, in the open, and under the stealthy cover of "company-sensitive" secret operations. This myriad of iterations demands a different kind of planning tool, one that conforms to a more realistic cycle of your book of business. So, it isn't that Plan, Brief, Execute, and Debrief won't work; it's that most of the time, it just doesn't fit a true picture of the business environment and therefore takes too much energy to work efficiently. By interrupting the "flow," you take people off of their game. Teams spend more time servicing the "process" than actually doing the j-o-b!

In business, my clients have this cycle moving around itself at all times. One project may be in a planning phase while another is in a debrief phase. One business problem stalls because it requires a step back to the planning phase during the execution phase and one project cannot afford to take the time to accomplish a comprehensive briefing phase. Moreover, in almost every case I have seen working with even the best and most efficient teams in the country, the willingness or ability to take a moment to accomplish a debrief is almost nonexistent. It was clear to me early on that the Plan, Brief, Execute, and Debrief model could work in business, but that the cultural and operational foundation of most businesses prevented an easy fit. I developed VECTOR to tailor a planning process to fill the void of space between and outside your normal business planning cycle when you are under pressure. Just like ACE, VECTOR requires cultivating a high-performance culture if it is to work effectively. *Check Six!* The objective as a unique planning tool is that when VECTOR is triggered and implemented, clear objectives are defined, an action team is assembled with key player's input, and several Plans of Action are developed to the point that decision makers can cut through the fog and friction of the environment and make a decision. VECTOR is a planning tool to give company leaders at least three Plans of Action (POA) from which to make a call and execute a plan. The best part is that VECTOR can overlay any planning tools your team utilizes, it thrives outside the normal business planning cycle, and anyone can do it!

These business-proven components make up the VECTOR process:

- ✓ **V**erify
- ✓ **E**valuate
- ✓ **C**oordinate and **C**ommunicate
- ✓ **T**ranslate and **T**ask
- ✓ **O**ffer Three Plans of Action (POAs)
- ✓ **R**eassess and **R**eview

VECTOR gives teams a unique and straightforward system to cope with high-pressure situations that affords a bit more time and has an impact above the tactical or operational level. It deals with implications of a strategic nature. The value of VECTOR is that, like ACE, it gives your team a formal, defined process to deal with business problems, rather than an ad hoc approach to operational issues. So, I think it is worth spending a moment examining how businesses typically handle out-of-cycle planning.

It is quite common for my clients to handle these types of business problems in a couple of different ways—most of which are not codified company standard operating procedure. First, companies tell teams to handle their "book of business," which means that if something outside of the normal planning process occurs, yielding a high-pressure situation, the team leaders tend to be their own. Others reassign their "star players" to the account to ensure that the business isn't lost or that customer satisfaction isn't damaged. Still others let everything in the division come to a grinding halt and through economies of scale, everyone is compelled to pitch in and lessen the blow of the situation at hand. I've developed a much more effective way to handle this type of high-pressure situation.

The problem with telling your team to "handle their book of business" on their own is that it tends to give a sense that they have no mutual support. The process I developed helps each other *Check Six!* No one should have to navigate a high-pressure situation alone. As a proponent of building a high-performance culture, your first imperative should be to construct processes that foster a sense of team and support. Sometimes, company leaders feel more comfortable reassigning their star players to a high-pressure situation. This isn't fair to the newly assigned team if it becomes a trend. It also kills the confidence of the team that is taken off the task. More importantly, it only treats the symptom, not the problem. At some point, the high-pressure situations presented will outnumber the star players you have. Moreover, your goal is to build a high-performance culture where every team member can work within the construct of stress. Another way to deal with these issues is to "stop the bus."

I see clients frequently use the "all hands on deck" approach and bumble from one high-pressure situation to another, much like a youth soccer team, with no concept of position or spacing, trudging after the ball like an amorphous life blob. This is impractical and leads to a situation where eventually companies suffer because teams have no time to think strategically. They are constantly embroiled in overwhelming tactical tasking. They exist to put out fires. At some point, companies using this method will violate the *"lose sight, lose fight"* axiom of a high-performance culture and the system will fail. It is like driving a car down the road at 100 miles per hour and having to change the tires. Inaction will lead to a blow out, but the car will crash if you try to change the tires at speed. Rarely can a company pull to the side and take the time to put on new rubber, but having a comprehensive process will allow your teams to slow to a manageable, safe speed, change the tires, and press on. When I worked with Eclipse Aviation in Albuquerque, New Mexico, their CEO, Vern Rayburn, told me, "We are great at putting out fires; the problem is we are even better at starting them!" Vern was describing a common problem in business today, known as "We can't get out of our own way!"

The first step in this process is to define the situations where this process will be used. In so doing, consider the difference between applying ACE and VECTOR. The emphasis in ACE is to deal with high-pressure situations having tactical implications of a rapid nature. VECTOR has strategic implications, and while it is stressful, teams have time to plan a response. Next, identify who on the team or in the company needs to be involved in this process. While ACE gives teams a process to handle pressure-packed situations, VECTOR is more strategic, and therefore will touch many other parts of the company. Then, define the process used to integrate your team's efforts. Use checklists and standard operating procedures in a standardized way to help teams feel comfortable in their approach to the problem. Ensure that this process can function within and alongside the regular business planning cycle—not replace it! A part of the process needs to be a means to assess the effectiveness in dealing with the challenge. This ensures that the process can be refined in subsequent high-pressure situations and learning can occur.

Defining when the VECTOR process is to be implemented is an important step in the process because it will serve as the trigger for a change in action. Having clear cut guidelines negates the confusion that a high-pressure situation brings and is directly in line with the notion of a high-performance culture. In a way, it becomes a standard operating procedure and propagates consistency. Defining and communicating these criteria gives your team a foundation from which clear, unambiguous action based on purpose will flow. Just as I define a high-pressure situation in broad terms with my clients, I ask them to take a big-picture approach to establishing guidelines for when the VECTOR process is to be used. The mindset is the same as ACE; in other words, I'd rather implement VECTOR, begin the process, and curtail it if not applicable, than to try to catch up to high-pressure challenges because we misidentified the real problem. When my clients ask, "When do we use it," some of the characteristic triggers I ask them to consider include:

- ✓ perceived pressure of the situation;
- ✓ potential for disproportionate upside or downside return on investment;
- ✓ short-lived opportunity;
- ✓ risk to critical market share or positioning.

Usually my clients come up with many more considerations, all of which are valid and specific to their explicit needs. The point is, in considering when VECTOR is triggered, the actions to deal with high-pressure situations, coupled with the list of characteristics above, are based upon carefully-thought-out plans and are not thrown together at the last minute in reaction to the event. Once the trigger is identified, take the time to identify what parts of the company must be involved with the process.

Some high-pressure situations require very centralized control and some can be guided more loosely. Having the correct subject matter experts (SMEs) on the team can have the effect of making the process flow easier or it can be the difference between success and failure. The challenge is to work the process with only those needed. At the same time, leverage subject matter experts so that you have all the bases covered. Stay in your lane! Some companies I work with use the trigger to pull SMEs off normal tasking and to form cells to deal with the issue at hand, and some just roll it into normal tasking but assign a higher priority. The great thing is that VECTOR works either way. Personally, I am more comfortable having the planning cell convened because it helps to focus efforts and sets the perception that whatever issue has triggered VECTOR is very important.

Use this process as a means to integrate action across the company. By pulling in legal, accounting, mid-level management, risk analysis, relationship managers, company leadership, and whomever else is appropriate, a comprehensive plan is produced. Integrating across the company gets people from different divisions talking and communicating. Good things happen when people in adjacent cubicles take the time to get to know and understand what others' roles in the company are and how they do business. I am amazed how many of my clients don't understand how their actions, minute as they may be, significantly affect their co-workers downstream. This awareness helps build a high performance culture.

This process supports the notion of centralized control and decentralized execution. It is the way we employ in the fighter jet business. The centralized control comes from the generals in charge of specifying the objectives of the campaign. They then count on us to apply the appropriate proportionate force and tactics in a decentralized way to get the job done. In the case of high-value assets, the opposite can be true.

In the most recent conflicts, one of the most effective modes of combat is the small, agile, and elite Special Forces groups that integrate movement and stealth into their operations. For them, the doctrine of centralized control and decentralized execution inhibits their ability to execute. The team itself is a high-value asset and as such, requires a better suited method. Groups like the Special Forces use a doctrine akin to decentralized control and centralized execution. They need the ability to work autonomously to be most effective for many reasons. First, the execution cycle time can be extremely compressed. They do not have time to wait for orders from above and then execute a plan. Second, the process of communication itself can forfeit any advantage they might have from working invisibly. Finally, the capability that the team brings to the fight is not suited for large-force employment and therefore requires some other order of battle. These Special Forces teams still have identified objectives, know the commander's intent, and understand their role in the bigger picture. They still take time to plan a mission in detail and they debrief. But in the aggregate, the doctrine needs to support the fight and vice versa. In business, most companies use a centralized control and decentralized execution model, whether they know it or not, to take advantage of efficiencies and economies of scale. However, in high-pressure situations, and within a high-performance culture, there may be times when your elite teams need the agility to execute in a different way. They need to understand completely the objective and then deploy in light, quick teams. For these teams, it may be better to execute with a decentralized control and centralized execution model. Just understand, those using this model have to be able to execute on a high level. Is your team prepared for this? As a leader in a stressful situation, you have to be sure your team is capable of handling the autonomy and is fully briefed on the components of a high-performance culture. Employing these methods is up to you. Realize that your team may or may not know the trigger has been tripped. It is up to you to say, "Go!" After the trigger is defined and the players are identified, it is time to start the VECTOR process.

- ✓ **V**erify
- ✓ **E**valuate
- ✓ **C**oordinate and **C**ommunicate
- ✓ **T**ranslate and **T**ask
- ✓ **O**ffer Three Plans of Action (POAs)
- ✓ **R**eassess and **R**eview

Many times, what on the surface appears to be a challenge or opportunity turns out to be neither when you shine the light of clarity on it. But as I have seen so many times in the business world, your aggressive team jumps in to a high-pressure situation without paying due diligence to defining reality, understanding the big picture, taking time to plan, and defining their piece of the pie. And even though it can be couched in the best of intentions, this is impulse, not purposeful execution. So the first thing a team must do in the VECTOR process is to VERIFY that the trigger has been met. Write it down! Explain in simple, clear terms why and how the trigger has been met. This will help you move to the next step and help spell out the purpose for moving forward. If you take some time at step one, you may find that the trigger indeed has not been met and the group is better suited to deal with the situation in the normal business planning cycle. This saves effort, resources, and facilitates the group understanding of what meets the threshold of a high-pressure situation. If you VERIFY the trigger has been met, quickly move to EVALUATE the environment and your objectives.

There are myriad considerations that need to be weighed in the EVALUATE phase, but just like any other process in a high-pressure situation, start by defining the objectives of the team. Perform a SWOT analysis (strengths, weaknesses, opportunities, and threats.) Realize that the VECTOR process is meant, in the end, to define three Plans of Action for team leaders to choose from, so you are not necessarily convened to solve a problem; rather, you are there to propose options. Having said that, your objectives should still conform to the high-performance culture model, meaning, they need to be specific, measurable, attainable, relevant, and timely. In the EVALUATE phase, begin by identifying the desired outcome and set the objectives. Ensure they are in line with the company's overall strategic and tactical plan, as well as in line with the vision of the organization. As a guide, use the characteristics of a high-pressure situation: Risk Level, Perception of Time, Expectations (perceived or real), Personal Expectations, Mutual Support, Ambiguity of Problem, Relative Outcome, Stress, Alignment of Skill Set, Access to Information, Experience, Attitude and Approach, Level of Responsibility and Accountability, Fear of Failure, and Training. This sets the stage and converts the data before you into information. Be as specific as possible. Classify the challenge and set a time horizon of when a desired result must be produced. Make the timeline a standardized period and make it aggressive! The timeline is dependent on the complexity of the problem, but again, make the timeline aggressive. Typically, the business problems confronted by VECTOR do not span long, extended periods. Rather, they present targets of opportunity upon which a business want to capitalize, or are high-pressure situations in which the company has no recourse but to find a way to execute...and NOW! Sometimes, my clients run VECTOR on a timeline of one day and sometimes of one quarter. The time span is part of the EVALUATION phase and it is expressed in the timeline you identify and broadcast to the team. Now that you have direction and an event horizon, you can communicate information and coordinate those SMEs that you need on the team.

Remember the adage about COMMUNICATION? No matter how many times you say something or how many ways you say it, 10% won't get the word! Don't forget that, when you are assembling your team. COORDINATE who needs to be in the room! Run down each division is to see if they must have input on the process. Always strive to include those players you need to be on the team, balanced against having too many voices. Streamline the team and pare it down to only those who can provide relevant input, or to those who, for subject matter expertise reasons, must have a speaking part on the team.

Begin by going through the list with a standardized briefing guide not only to be more efficient, but also to strive to employ in a standardized manner. Explain why the trigger for VECTOR was met, lay the groundwork with the Evaluation process, including specific objectives, and then communicate your intentions. The goal is, as always, to come up with three POAs for company leaders to choose from within the allotted time. Strive to complete this phase of planning, knowing that everyone is on the same sheet of music. This will provide a consistent place from which to start and is a tenet of a high-performance culture. With this goal in mind, do the hard work when communicating: translate the data into a format of information that everyone on the team, regardless of the area of expertise, can understand and process. This probably is old news to you, but for a variety of reasons, different divisions within your company speak different languages! I was given this education once when I did a series of seminars for William Lyon Homes in California.

The first seminar I gave was to their Warranty Group. These were the people on the front lines of the home sales engagement. Their role was to complete the walk-through with the new home owner once the home was complete. More importantly, for the subsequent six months, they would be the point of contact for any of the inevitable problems arising in a new home. Daily, they'd handle calls like, "There is water coming out of my wall!" Never a good scene! At Lyon Homes, some of their most gifted workers delicately navigated the minefield of the Warranty Division. It was amazing. My techniques on handling high-pressure situations resonated with them because they had seen, heard, and felt it all! They had one pet peeve. This nagging challenge was not the needy new-home-owning clients; it was the sales people they had problems with—their own coworkers. This totally surprised me!

"They overpromise," one warranty person said.

"They say one thing but mean something else," another added.

I noted their frustration and took these to my next seminar with the sales force.

William Lyon Homes was in a boom in the mid-2000s. They were selling houses as fast as they could make them—even faster in some cases! The sales force was well-trained, knowledgeable, and as good as I had worked with in my time as a consultant. After speaking with them during my seminar, I asked them if they "ever overpromised," or if they "ever said one thing but meant another"? Of course, they denied, denied, denied any culpability! Still, it was clear to me what was going on: warranty and sales were speaking different languages. No one group was right and no group was wrong. This divergence had developed over time in response to the incredible pressure that Sales felt in turning over houses, and the high stress that Warranty had in dealing with the pressure of having to be expert on every potential problem in a new home. Luckily, the answer was fairly straightforward. I got the groups together and we translated. We ran real scenarios and practiced communicating in a standardized way. We took into account both Sales and Warranty's needs, as well as the needs of the inexperienced client. Just as importantly, we took into account the goals, vision, and objectives of the company. Lyon Homes had done the difficult part in taking the time to develop a high-performance culture. All I had to do was to translate between the divisions to get them communicating. The results were immediate and quantifiable. We have to do the same thing in aviation.

We use standardized terms that have been translated so that no matter whether you are flying a Censsna-152 at 100 knots or an F-15 at 650 knots, the communication works and the real message is translated and conveyed. This makes aviation a very safe, effective, and efficient endeavor. We have to use this standardized method of communication because even though we are all just "flying," our aircraft travel at vastly different speeds, have vastly different capabilities, and go to vastly different places. Wow! Sounds like the capabilities of your company's teams! No matter what airfield I am flying to, five miles from the end of the runway, when I am on final approach, I am required to announce, "Tiger 1, 5 miles, gear down, full stop," to tell everyone I am landing.

I do this flying into Incirlik Air Base in Turkey in my F-15 and I do this flying into O'Hare International Airport, Chicago in my 737. It is the standard. It is the standard for a lot of reasons. First, it reports my position. Second, it cues me to complete my pre-landing checklist. Finally, it lets everyone else know exactly where to look to find me and takes a variable out of the dynamic flying environment. It is a simple process yet it applies universally—brilliant! Still, it only works if we are on the same radio frequency.

You be the translator! Consult with trusted team members in the TRANSLATE and TASK phase. Be aware that you cannot translate all of the work done in the preceding phases without knowing the language your other team members speak. If possible, leave nothing to interpretation. While, in a perfect world, you could skip this phase, acknowledge that a little effort translating now will pay dividends in the heat of a high-pressure situation. Leave the debrief for questions like "how can we make this a smoother process?" Next, parse the action plan to the members on the team. TASK team members with specific deliverables and set the expectation. Now that everyone is on the same sheet of music, you can move as one team to the most important phase of VECTOR—Offer Three Plans of Action.

You have spent a lot of time developing the culture of leaders at every level of your organization; after all, it is the force multiplier in a high-performance culture. Now is where you get to see the payoff! Be cognizant of the fact that your team's objective is not to make the decisions for the CEO and COO; it is to offer them plans of action so that they can make informed decisions for the company. Make no mistake; they are counting on your expertise and knowledge.

Don't spend time trying to solve the challenge, but concentrate your efforts on giving company leaders actionable plans that produce results and can be implemented as soon as they say, "go!" The three unique Plans of Action can have different desired effects, but they must all support the overall objectives. This is easily the most complex phase of the VECTOR process, so as a leader at your level, ensure that you stick to the timeline identified in the Evaluate phase. There is an old fighter pilot adage I share with my clients in this phase: the mission planning cycle takes the allotted time plus another 10 minutes. If you have four hours in this phase, no matter how simple the task, the planning phase will take four hours and 10 minutes! The reason this has become an immutable law of business planning is simple. We all want to produce the perfect product. I want my team to have this mindset while understanding that in a high-pressure situation, the timeline takes precedence over perfection. I have seen it a million times in the business world, and I repeat: even a mediocre plan executed well is better than no plan at all (and no plan at all is what you'll produce if you miss the timeline!). It is imperative that your team keeps continuity by working through all three POAs; if they cannot, it is likely that you will have to backtrack through the preceding phases to get everyone back on task. POAs must be clear and unambiguous. They need to be easily explainable and must be the basis for execution. They should be specific and produce a measurable, purposeful outcome based on meeting the objective. Once you have created three POAs, package them clearly and send them up the chain. Be ready to field questions and provide data. Make sure you are ready to address the concerns of company leaders as they begin the task of choosing the POA they wish to execute. After you have handed off your product, you can begin the last phase of the process, even though you can't complete it until the POA chosen has run its course.

The final phase of the VECTOR process, REASSESS and REVIEW, allows teams to look inward to refine the process and identify the lessons learned. Focus on the objectives and the process itself so that personalities don't bog down the discussion. Admittedly, this is a lot easier said than done! Even though VECTOR is still in force, there is time to look inward in order to garner the lessons on how to make VECTOR better, faster, and more foolproof for your team. Make sure the lessons are documented and kept in a place where they are accessible for the next time the VECTOR trigger is met. Concentrate on how you can fix, modify, and customize the process for your team. Keep one eye on the POAs as well; you may be called on to clarify and decipher plans for the decision makers. *Check Six!* Have a plan to reconvene when the POA has been chosen, implemented, and produced the desired effect. After that, get back together and reassess the entire VECTOR process, this time including the outcome. Use this time to keep to the big-picture items and don't be tempted to rehash old news. Still, be aware that when you do a root cause analysis of the entire process, some of the problems may have been internal to the team, so they must be addressed. The difference is that in the REVIEW phase, you are looking at how the team worked on an administrative level and in the REASSESS phase, you are looking at how the team met its objective based upon its purposeful execution. Focus on "what" went right and wrong, not "who" did right and wrong. When these lessons are identified, document them and put them in a place readily accessible for the next time.

The VECTOR process is the best way to provide your company leaders with the information and plans they need to execute. It requires that your high-performance culture exercises leadership at every level of the organization, and challenges communication flow and produces results based on purpose. Always remember that your team objective is to provide three POAs, not to solve the problem. Let the solution come from whichever appropriate POA is implemented. This process is meant to be started as soon as the criterion is triggered. It gives your team a simple process to use during a high-pressure situation when you have time to plan, but find yourself out of the normal planning cycle. Remember that old saying, "If you fail to prepare, you are preparing to fail."

Both in the dynamic, pressure-packed ACE situations and the high-pressure out-of-cycle planning VECTOR situations, you will be called upon to be a leader at your appropriate level. So, let me ask you this: have you ever taken the time to clearly identify what kind of leader you are? Were you born a leader, or have you taken the time over your professional development to become a leader? Do you want to lead? What is your leadership style? In working with some of the most gifted, up-and-coming military and business leaders, I have found that one thing consistently emerges when I ask this question: most people aren't truly sure how to answer because they haven't either taken or had the time to consider these issues—they are too busy executing! Let's break that cycle!

10

The Leader:
Being "In Front" in High-Pressure Situations

"Find those people who provide the direction, energy, and drive that shape outcomes, not those who react skillfully to a series of events."

—Anon

X. The Leader: Being "In Front" in High Pressure Situations

In the months following the tragedy of September 11, 2001, I was amazed at the stories of heroism, human kindness, and compassion that permeated the lexicon of the community. Stories of those forfeiting safety and wellbeing for the sake of others in the World Trade Center slowly trickled into the public awareness. I grappled with difficulty to define my place in it all. For the first time since I had been on Cape Cod, people perceived a change in consciousness. It seemed there was an elegant aftereffect of this completely high-pressure situation and the true human spirit was coaxed from its slumber. It was remarkable to see it again. Buried in the tedium of day-to-day life, the toil to get ahead, and the superfluous tabloid news, was this infinitesimal yet unquenchable life force shattering the calmness and indifference that had become the hallmark of our society. When reflecting on how different life had become, a dirge permeated my serenity. I wondered how long this would last. I already lamented the day of its departure. But for today, it was time to look at life with a slightly different hue. It was time to notice things and time to slow down. It was time to reprioritize the important things and stifle the minutia. After all, those who perished in World Trade Center 1 and World Trade Center 2 had just simply gone to work on September 11th. Those who lost their lives on United 93 did not ask for the chance to be heroes. On the morning of departure for those on United 175, passengers did not ask to be on the front lines of the war on terrorism. So it was that life had changed. Some longed for a change and others disdained change, but change came nonetheless.

Among other deeply life-changing things, for me, September 11, 2001 codified a principle I guess I had discovered in preparing for the most high-pressure situations in both my military and civilian business career. High-pressure situations shake out who the real leaders are. If you can take the blame out of the system and focus on the objectives, if you can spotlight accountability and remove innuendo, you can begin to apply a litmus test to your leadership ability in stressful situations. A perfect example of this was the 9/11 Commission charged with debriefing the attack on our country. For those of us involved in the tragedy, it was obvious early on that politics and positioning were the true objective for the commission. It was disappointing and it was obvious as soon as the commission members were named.

Put the techniques I teach in your "bag of tricks.". As long as there is a healthy dose of candidness and a sincere willingness to do the work to get better, and prepare, I am sure that anyone can handle stressful situations skillfully. So it makes sense, as we complete our conversation on leadership, to leave you with a place to start when you put this book down. I've given you a career's worth of information to consider in a short presentation. At some point, when this book is just your *most* valued adviser prominently perched in your bookcase collecting dust, use this chapter as a departure point to define your personal style of leadership in high-pressure situations.

Are leaders born? Are leaders made? What is a leader? What class helped you define your leadership style? I teach my clients that the role of leadership is to create the conditions for superiors, peers, and subordinates to succeed. Sometimes this is not an easy task. Think about it: in order for you to create the conditions for your boss to succeed, you have to be willing to also let someone else take the credit. Normally, people will give credit where credit is due, but this is not always the case. Still, I find in the end analysis, at some point, the truth will come out, no matter what the situation. I usually get push back with this concept. Generally, team players understand and agree that their role is to lay the groundwork for subordinates to succeed. They also understand the *Check Six* concept and assist their peers, but their superiors? That's a different story. I challenge them to break through that emotional barrier. Help everyone on the team reach new levels of development and performance and do it with attitude. Most of the time, my clients are reluctant. They are aggressive, fast movers with their sights set on moving up the ladder in the company. They want credit and they want to succeed. For those people, I offer my father's words of encouragement. He said, "Life is a big sine wave, and in the end, it all evens out." It's akin to saying, "You can't take it with you!" It's true. Stay honest to yourself and your principles, and in the end, you will get the recognition you deserve. It may not be in the same business unit or even in the same company, but when people see you, let them say that you are a team player and not afraid to do the job without thinking about who gets the credit. Trust me: over the course of your body of work, the truth will show.

I have read many books attempting to define leadership. They always impel me to pick the definition apart and apply some anecdote from my business or military experience to disprove it, at least in part. Rather than getting caught in the pitfall of applying a definition to leadership, I challenge you to define it. Once you have, ask yourself how leadership in a high-pressure situation is different. Is it different?

Here's a good start to a definition of leadership: Leadership is the ability to influence—a simple six-word description. When I coach clients, we start by picking apart this definition to personalize it for them. I start by identifying the traits, principles, and vision of leaders that they admire. This gives a good basis from which to start to define the type of leader they see in themselves. I focus the topic by bounding discussion around leadership style, rather than focusing on the definition of leadership itself. Leave the definition to the PhDs and the research assistants and the ivory towers. Rather, define what leadership means to you and what kind of leader you want to be.

Everyone has some ability to lead because everyone is born with leadership traits. So, back to my original question, in this sense, leaders are born. The extent to which one exhibits leadership behavior varies from person to person, but make no mistake: everyone possesses these traits to some degree. This discussion is not rocket science. I bring them to the table because they not only are the basis for good leadership, but they are also the basis to a happy life and support the three tenets of a fighter pilot (*Speed Is Life; Lose Sight, Lose Fight; Check Six*).

When you isolate leadership in a high-pressure situation, I have found that effective leaders lean on these traits even more than in normal leadership situations, or at least, in a more overt, purposeful way. Think about it: how many times in a crisis have you seen someone's true colors come out—for good or for bad? This usually results from someone acting on impulse. It is not to say that people don't make mistakes, or act irrationally under stress, but at some point, what you see is what you get— positive or negative.

For a leader to be consistently effective in a high-pressure situation, he or she must exhibit these behaviors: integrity, honesty, commitment, proactiveness, and selflessness. When the fog and friction of the business battlefield hits unexpectedly, these traits are the pillars for action. They are your base. If you develop these traits when no one is looking, you will find that in the fog and friction of battle they will blossom and shine—and people will notice.

Integrity is essential to foster a sense of respect from your team members. Strive to maintain the highest professional standards, too. Then take it a step further and maintain the highest personal standards. As a leader, you may find yourself living life in a fishbowl sometimes. Don't be intimidated by this; it is natural. Rather, be aware of it and use it as a vehicle to demonstrate the integrity you have. Once your team knows that you have integrity, they become comfortable performing at the edge of their personal envelope. I learned the lesson of integrity early on in life from the best man I've ever known: my father. Our task one day was to run by the supermarket and pick up some miscellaneous groceries for my mother. It was going to be a high-speed pass, so I jumped in the passenger seat, strapped in, and off we went. I scurried around the store collecting the items my father asked me to find. We rejoined at the checkout and unloaded our haul. To save room in the cart, my father had loaded the large water jug on the bottom, just under the basket and over the flailing wheels. It could have just as well been loaded in the infinity of a black hole because we wanted out of the store fast and because it fell below our line of sight! When we rolled the cart and arrived at the car, I unloaded the groceries into the car with the care of an airline baggage handler. Just then my dad made a noise. He had forgotten to load the water on to the belt to be added to the bill. I said, "Oh, well, no big deal," as he shut the doors and locked the car.

"What are you doing, dad?"

"I am going back in to pay, son. Let's go," he responded.

"It no big deal, they don't even know," I retorted.

"It is a big deal." He continued, "My integrity is not for sale, so let's go back in and pay."

We went back in and paid. I revisit that simple lesson on integrity more times than I care to admit in my daily life. It has served me well. The next step is to be honest with them, because they are watching all the time.

Honesty goes hand-in-hand with integrity. Where honesty is concerned, the stakes are incredibly high. I have worked with men and women in the "C" suite of corporations who have worked all of their professional careers to build integrity by being honest in the good and the bad times, only to trade it all away for one moment of expediency. The expectation on your team has to be that everyone is honest or it will cause friction. I hear my clients say over and over again, "I can handle bad news, I just can't handle fiction." Honesty is an imperative. In a high-pressure situation, the demand for honesty increases and your team cannot execute if they don't know you are *checking their six!* Realize that honesty is a two-way street. If you give honesty at all costs, then you are entitled to expect honesty in return. Once your team understands you to be an honest person, they will offer a sign of trust—commitment.

Commitment begins by understanding the mission and your role. Communicate the role of the team members so that you are on the same sheet of music. Next, demonstrate your commitment by executing. Commitment to the mission requires that your team acknowledges commitment to the superiors who ultimately will evaluate success or failure. Just as importantly, it requires commitment to your subordinates in the trenches who are working hard to get the job done. A high-performance culture fosters a mindset where commitment is the hallmark and it will be the concept that fuels high-performance execution. But to execute a peak performance, your team can't just wait to field the curve balls that a high-pressure situation throws at them. Your team must be in front of those curve balls, anticipating the upcoming changes and planning for them.

Proactiveness accelerates high-performance execution. Be the kind of leader who takes the initiative and acts before a challenge turns into a crisis. In doing so, acknowledge the responsibility that comes along with the task and, just like anything else in your high-performance culture, accept the responsibility with confidence. If you can't be completely confident in yourself, be confident in your team. A proactive mindset will enable you to maintain the bias for action that a high-pressure situation calls for. It will inevitably also ask you to subordinate your own personal agenda to the needs of the team at some point.

A high-pressure situation usually demands that team members work together at a high performance level. This means that, whether you like it or not, you may have to stem the urge to put your needs above the team. If you can exhibit selfless behavior and do this successfully, it will spotlight the other leadership traits that you have worked so hard to develop. Make the right decision for the team in a high-pressure situation. Put trust in your supervisors to take care of you and put your team members in the limelight. This is not easy, especially if your team is made up of self-serving egoists. But if you approach the task selflessly, people will notice. Some days you will do this better than others, and that's okay. Just know that selflessness is the last leadership trait I discuss with my clients because it is the most difficult to show consistently.

Here's the bottom line: Leadership traits won't matter if you can't execute. Live the traits you espouse and show them in your behavior. In a high-pressure situation, these traits will draw attention to the kind of leader you are and they will be your foundation. How do you project the leadership traits you were born with? How much time do you spend debriefing yourself on these traits? What are you doing right now to develop these traits so that they are primed and ready when you find yourself in a high-pressure situation? Once you assess where you are as a leader, based upon the traits you have, it is time to get "in the weeds" and apply the traits you have to the leadership principles of a high-pressure situation.

The principles of leadership are your canvas upon which to paint a beautiful picture. The extent to which you develop those principles is up to you. While an impressionist Monet painting is certainly a beautiful work of art, in high-pressure leadership situations, you may seek a style with more clarity! I impress upon my clients that these principles are what require constant honing. They are where you set yourself apart as a leader and they are spotlighted in a high-pressure situation. They are:

- ✓ Know your job;
- ✓ Know yourself;
- ✓ Communicate;
- ✓ Motivate.

The goals and vision of your company are set from the top and flow down through planning groups, the "C" suite, and managers. The challenge is to find your piece of the pie. Once you know what is expected of you and how you contribute to the overall objectives, it is up to you to implement and execute. To be able to complete your task, which is essential to the overall success of the company, you have to know your job inside and out. I always scoff a bit when managers ask their team to "think outside the box." I never ask my team to think outside the box. I use my leadership vision to innovate and that responsibility lies at my level. I want my team to concentrate on getting the job done, especially in a high-pressure situation. To that end, I don't ask my wingmen to think outside the box, I ask them to think inside the box, just differently.[21] There is a big difference.

In a high-pressure situation, I depend on my team to execute at an extremely high level. I need them to focus on their piece of the task and produce results. It is a tactical endeavor. So, thinking outside of the box tends to encourage them to leave their skill set behind as they ponder innovation. Make no mistake: innovation is critical. But I encourage my team to stay inside the box (their skill set), and just take a different approach. This motivates them to assess their own ability to innovate and bounds them by their specific strengths and the needs of the high-pressure situation. It is a productivity enhancer and, in my experience, produces a result based on purpose rather than guesses. Taking a new approach to a task is fine, but we want to fight our fight, we want to be on our timeline, we want to ACE the situation rather than be aced. The best way to do this is to stay in the box, just think about the box differently. So no matter the approach you decide to take, you must start by understanding the tactical objectives that your leaders present.

Even in a high-pressure situation, I constantly ask myself, "How are we doing in relation to our objectives?" This keeps me focused as a leader and helps the team understand where they

---

[21] Sam Samsel

are in relation to the big picture. Align the company's vision and goals with the strategic objectives and then give your team clear, specific, tactical objectives and the effect will be amazing. It breaks down like this: the goals and vision provide the direction, the strategic objectives provide the quantifiable standard, and the tactical objectives give your team the roadmap by which to get there. It is, in and of itself, a process to enhance productivity and a tool to manage effort, resources, and expectations. I find that clients tend to lose their focus in a high-pressure situation because they don't understand clearly the expectation—so define it!

Always look for the opportunity to set the standard. It gives your team a bar to shoot for. It also enhances learning in the debrief because it gives you a place to start. You can point out specific examples of an individual's falling short of the standard, instruct them on how to meet the standard, and then give them the resources they need to exceed the standard next time. A good place to start is to always set the example.

Leadership by example is a simple concept. In the military, you often hear leaders say, "I'd never ask my team to do something I wouldn't do myself." Really? I understand the sentiment, but maybe the team is better than the leader at a specific task! That's okay! I frame it like this: I depend on my team to get the job done because sometimes I CAN'T DO IT MYSELF! I need someone *checking my six!* Where I can lead by example is not in the tactical execution necessarily, but in the approach I take to the task and the enthusiasm I bring to the mission. I go back to the leadership principles and THAT is where I can set the example.

In order to lead by example, I need to know my strengths and drive the fight towards those strengths. In a high-pressure situation, this technique is overlooked because people let themselves become a victim of the situation. Also, going into a situation with your eyes open and a realistic expectation necessitates knowing and acknowledging your weaknesses. When I consult with companies across the country and I ask them to write down their weaknesses, most can do it with the ease of a canned job interview. But then I ask them if they acknowledge their weaknesses and how, I get the Eddie Murphy in *Trading Places* response: "I am a karate man, karate man don't show their weaknesses, karate man keep their weakness on the inside." Why? Here's another newsflash: most on your team already know your weaknesses, or they are going to find out in a high-pressure situation. Be honest and ask for help. Acknowledging your weaknesses gives you permission to seek input and then enables you to begin to trust the decisions that you are going to have to make in the heat of the battle.

When you are asking for input, realize that you have to listen for what is being said and for what is not being said. Sometimes the absence of words speaks volumes. This is not the time to build barriers to communication nor is it time to keep secrets. Being a leader in a high-pressure situation necessitates constant attention to communication. It isn't always easy, but speak with candor when candor is called for. Share the knowledge you have and be confident in knowing that many times your team can handle the bad news; they just can't handle the void created by no news. Trust me; they will fill that void with rumor and innuendo.

The actions that you take in during a high-pressure situation are constantly being evaluated by your team. Rest on your leadership principles, and develop your leadership traits. I always tell my clients that if they want to lead, it is up to them to make their team want to follow. Find what motivates your team to get the job done. It is probably different for each team member. For some, it will be money, for some, it will be time off, some will even surprise you with their motivating factor, but as a leader, figure it out right now so that when a high-pressure situation presents itself, you know exactly where to go to motivate your team. Recognize excellence in public, and critique in private. This is a "leadership 101" principle, right, but in high-pressure situations, you'd be surprised how many times this one slips out and people are harshly critiqued on the spot. Don't forget: you are a leader, you are driving the fight; don't lose your composure due to stress. Share your enthusiasm for the task by showing how badly you want to hit it out of the park! It very well may be that the high pressure that comes with the task demotivates your team and allows a sense of defeat to permeate. This is natural. Breathe through your nose three times and hack a clock! Figure out the next step and then put some energy behind it; it will spread throughout the team. Never forget that someone is *checking your six!*

Empower your subordinates and challenge them to be leaders at their level. Use the high-performance culture to let your team run with it and execute. Remember, you are the leader and so you can delegate responsibility, but you can never delegate accountability. Monitor the situation, but let your team execute! In a high-pressure situation, you maintain control without micromanaging by providing the vision that the team needs, not by doing every task.

Leadership vision is something that comes with experience. It is the culmination of many wins and many losses. Experience gives you confidence because it becomes your database for action. This is exactly why, in a high-pressure situation, most leaders feel unprepared because they can't match experience with knowledge in their database. On September 11, 2001, because the situation was so chaotic and dynamic, in the air we made it look like something we had seen before. It was the only way we could get our arms around the enormity of the event. I am sure you've had the same feeling in business. As a leader, using your leadership vision is critical to giving your team the direction it needs to execute under stress. Give the team the VECTOR it needs.

As the person driving the fight, it is up to you to set the tactical objective, establish the timeline, and LEAD! Help your team maintain its perspective and be there to guide them. Be aware that micromanagement will slow progress and hinder innovation. As the leader in a high-pressure environment, your team will look to you for direction, consistency, and motivation. Knowing this, you can prepare for this type of leadership beforehand. Once your team feels grounded on the path you've set, you will become a crutch for them. They will reference your leadership and use it to anticipate what you want and how you'll react. Take a look at the next series of pictures and ask yourself, who is in the lead?

If you've ever been to an air show and seen the Thunderbirds, you recognize this signature maneuver called the "diamond." Here, Thunderbird 1, the flight lead, is at the pointy end of the spear: he is out in front and serves as the formation's lead. The wingmen are flying a specific position in relation to his jet, so he has to be smooth, consistent, and precise. In this picture, Thunderbird 1 is in the lead.

In this picture, who is in the lead? As you can see, a couple of the jets have left the formation in order to set up for a different maneuver. Still, the wingman needs a reference from which to fly. In this case, the jet on the left and in front is the leader. His wingmen are counting on him to lead them through the maneuver and get them where they need to be.

Now, who is leading in this picture? Anyone? Even though my friend Abner, Thunderbird 5, is solo, it can be said he is leading himself. This statement denotes a mindset that we cultivate in a high-performance culture. Think about it: in the first picture, Thunderbird 1 leads the entire formation. The wingmen fly in relation to his jet. But, if the wingmen don't practice leadership at their own level, they pose a danger to the group. If, as in this picture, Abner doesn't lead at his level, he could hit one of his wingmen during the diamond formation. If he doesn't lead at his level, the integrity of the formation is compromised. Thunderbird 1 is in control of the group in the first picture, but he counts on all of his wingmen to *"check his six"* for safety's sake and for the sake of the success of the mission. In a high-performance culture, we want leaders to be making decisions at their appropriate level, commensurate with their responsibility level and tasking. Once this mindset permeates a corporate culture, the level of execution will reach heights never imagined before—especially during high-pressure situations. Your vision as the overall leader is what will set the tone for execution.

As I mentioned before, a perfunctory task as the leader in a high-pressure situation is to provide vision through establishing the tactical objective. This is a critical step in preparation and offers a roadmap for success in high-pressure situations. It affords the group a way to visualize the steps in front of them to achieve the mission objective. It also helps the group to be as efficient as possible by giving them a means to gauge where priorities will fall during the execution phase. As the leader, this is your way to help scope the perspective.

In a high-pressure situation, it is important that your team is able to focus on the task at hand. You cannot, nor should you, try to fix everything! Deal in the moment with the stressful task in front of you and then take the lessons that you learn after the fact to move forward. As a leader, one of the most difficult things to do is to help your team maintain its perspective during periods of stress.

Try to suppress emotions and be patient with personalities. Use the tactical objectives as the anchor. If you focus on the objectives, then it is easier to focus on "what" is right or wrong, not "who" is right or wrong. In a high-pressure situation, the leader must be ready to correct to standards immediately to keep the team on track. Always prioritize tasks for your team and communicate your expectations. Don't be comfortable saying, "We need this step completed by the end of the week." Rather, say, "This step must be completed by 11 a.m. on Thursday. Questions?"

More than any other time, someone has to lead in a high-pressure situation. If you are that leader, providing the vision and direction for your team is the first and most important task. Leave your ego at home and be the one at the "pointy end of the spear." Empower your team to lead at its appropriate level. Working together, even the highest-pressure situations and most overwhelming stress can be overcome, handled, and capitalized on! Think about how impressed your clients will be when you handle these stressful situations in stride. Use that ability to further business development opportunities. Use ACE if you find yourself "in the moment" and you have to execute now. Use VECTOR if you have some time to plan and to consider several plans of action to attack a business challenge or opportunity.

Leadership, especially in high-pressure situations, is not easy. Leading takes practice and preparation. So let's reflect on the questions at the beginning of this chapter: are leaders born, or are leaders made? The answer is (drum roll, please) "Yes!" We are all born with the traits to be a great leader. We must develop, practice, and hone the principles of leadership under pressure. Finally, we must take the traits and principles to a new level by developing leadership vision for our team, our company, and our industry. At the "graduate" level of leadership, stressful situations provide the opportunity to leave your positive mark on the organization. Accept these situations with confidence and don't be intimidated. Set the objective, cultivate a high-performance culture, and let your team produce the results that the company needs.

The art of leadership is much like an air-to-air engagement in the F-15 Eagle: every single situation is dynamic and different. Anticipate the learning points to come from a comprehensive debrief. Look back on events as they transpired, then try to take the emotional responses out and see how you did in relation to the objective in front of you. If you can't drill down to the root causes of the outcomes you see, ask someone for input.

As you continue with me to the closing short chapter, it is time to answer, the question "so what?" One of my most successful clients would repeat this refrain for every technique and principle I taught his financial advisors. His persistent, terse, "southie"[22] inquiries are where we will end this discussion because I want to help you use ACE and VECTOR at your desk tomorrow.

---

[22] The southern section of Boston; its residents are known for their rather straightforward, unambiguous communication style!

11

The Debrief

"Progress cannot occur until reality is defined."

—Sam Samsel

XI. The Debrief: Soloing

One thing is consistent and spans both my military and business careers: in the absence of a plan during a high-pressure situation, events conspire to take on a life of their own and leave you in the tattered aftermath. During this process, your vision of the challenge ahead is clouded by the fog and friction created by the stressful situation. In an unfailing process of devolution, information reduces to data and team members exhibit uncharacteristic behaviors. Sometimes team members find their stride and shine, while others morph into an arid, faceless shell of themselves. The situation exists on its own timeline. I want you to ACE any high-pressure situation so that you can attain the goals you've set, if appropriate. Conversely, I want you to take charge and give your company's leaders a VECTOR from which to proceed. So what's next?

My sincere challenge to you is to put these techniques into practice wherever you think they fit. I use them in my professional life as well as in my personal life. I use ACE when I am confronted with a high-pressure situation at work for which I had not fully prepared, and I use it at home when my furnace decides it's had enough at the most inopportune time. ACE was developed to employ in high-pressure tactical situations. I use the VECTOR process in the same way, only differently!

VECTOR is a planning process for high-pressure situations. It deals more on the strategic level and is optimized for situations occurring out of your normal business planning cycle. I use VECTOR when a business opportunity develops requiring action in the near term, but includes the luxury of a window of time for planning. I also use VECTOR in my personal life when the wheels have come off my monthly budget, but there is still time and resources to develop an effective recovery plan. Both ACE and VECTOR have something very important in common: they are both simple. The challenge to you is that they are not easy to employ—that is, unless you use them assiduously, with discipline and consistency. Don't worry; I won't leave you hanging! *Check Six.*

The "so what" is this: even in the most stress-filled, hair-raising, pressure-packed, tension-filled situations, the outcome is in your hands. There is no mysterious process that responds to random external inputs. YOU CAN CONTROL the situation, but you MUST take a clear, methodical approach to a high-pressure situation. If on a tactical, execution level, then use ACE as your tool. If you have a challenge or opportunity outside of your normal business cycle but still have the time to plan, use VECTOR.

I can help your team with this process. I can show you that this works and that anyone can lead under pressure. My dynamic interactive seminars and keynotes will get you there! Check out the details on my web site: www.pureverticalconsulting.com. There, you can check out my blog and my podcasts. My objective is to show your team members that with a high-performance culture, ACE, and VECTOR, leadership under pressure is not intimidating; it is just a state of being. In my Leadership Development Forums, I will also help them discover what leadership means to them, as well as discovering and defining their own leadership style.

Every self-respecting fighter pilot has developed some sort of shorthand or "cheat sheet" as a crutch for operations. I believe this is because we are checklist-driven people, and this method is just another manifestation of a checklist. In order to jump-start your ability to solo (*Speed is Life*), this simple concluding chapter can be your crutch. Use it as a cheater to give these techniques a try. It will keep you on track so that you can be an effective, successful leader and produce purposeful results in any high pressure situation! As we say before every training engagement in fighter aviation (and with attitude!!) –

"Fight's On!"

*   *   *

Three Axioms
- Speed is Life
- Lose Sight, Lose Fight
- Check Six

*   *   *

ACE
1. **A**bate the threat.
2. **C**ontrol the situation
3. **E**valuate follow-on actions and **EXECUTE**

*   *   *

* * *

VECTOR
- ✓ **V**erify
- ✓ **E**valuate
- ✓ **C**oordinate and **C**ommunicate
- ✓ **T**ranslate and **T**ask
- ✓ **O**ffer Three Plans of Action (POAs)
- ✓ **R**eassess and **R**eview

* * *

The Foundation of a High Performance Culture
- – Focus
- – Attitude
- – Communication
- – Training
- – Support

* * *

www.scrambledthebook.com

Martin Richard is a combat fighter pilot, business consultant, and author. In his distinguished career, he has flown over 3,000 hours in the F-15 and F-111 fighter jets. Before becoming an author, Martin co-founded Fighter Associates, a business consulting group and worked with some of the largest (and smallest) companies in the country. His experience also includes flying for one of the world's largest civilian airline companies.

Today, Martin is a thought expert on leadership and a sought after public speaker. His experience in extremely high pressure situations and the tools he has developed to thrive in these circumstances resonates with America's best and brightest business leaders and delivers quantifiable results!

Don't wait! Contact him today at

www.scrambledthebook.com

SPEED IS LIFE!

4730380R0

Made in the USA
Charleston, SC
08 March 2010